MORE

THAN

ME

THE 4 ESSENTIALS OF
RELATIONAL WHOLENESS

MORE
THAN
ME

Jim　　　　　**Glenn**　　　　　**David**
Petersen　　**McMahan**　　　**Russ**

NAVPRESS●

NAVPRESS ⬤

NavPress is the publishing ministry of The Navigators, an international Christian organization and leader in personal spiritual development. NavPress is committed to helping people grow spiritually and enjoy lives of meaning and hope through personal and group resources that are biblically rooted, culturally relevant, and highly practical.

For a free catalog go to www.NavPress.com
or call 1.800.366.7788 in the United States or 1.800.839.4769 in Canada.

Library of Congress Cataloging-in-Publication Data

Petersen, Jim.
  More than me : the 4 essentials of relational wholeness / Jim Petersen, David Russ, and Glenn McMahan.
    p. cm.
  Includes bibliographical references.
  ISBN-13: 978-1-60006-265-0
  ISBN-10: 1-60006-265-2
  1. Interpersonal relations--Religious aspects--Christianity. I. Russ, David, 1958- II. McMahan, Glenn, 1962- III. Title.
  BV4597.52.P48 2008
  248.4--dc22

                        2008021388

Printed in the United States of America

1 2 3 4 5 6 7 8 / 11 10 09 08

CONTENTS

PREFACE

This book is the product of a relationship. It reflects the thinking, experiences, and personalities of three different men
working as a team. Because each of us has different strengths
and weaknesses, we believe that the outcome is stronger than if
the book had been written by just one person.

Jim developed the vision for the book and its scriptural
foundations. The author of numerous other books, Jim is gifted
at finding in Scripture relevant insights into cultural dilemmas.
The idea of this book was born from his personal observations
of the relational struggles that so many people face today. With
these observations in mind, Jim plunged into the Scriptures
and developed what we call the four essentials for relational
wholeness.

Then Jim invited me (Glenn) to join him in the project. When
the invitation came, I had been working with Brazilian university students for about eleven years, helping them prepare for
marriage, vocational life, and spiritual growth after college.
Because I had worked as a print journalist before moving to
Brazil, Jim invited me to do all the writing, to take the ideas and
put them into my own words.

Early in the process, Jim began to discuss his ideas with
several people, including David. At that time, David provided
Jim with some extensive notes based on his many years of helping people at his counseling center. Soon after, Jim came to

Brazil so that he and I could develop a specific outline. As we discussed our plans, we realized that David's ideas and observations would be important additions. So we decided to invite David to be a coauthor. He added a rich layer of understanding about human nature and relationships to our discussion.

The writing process has, for the most part, been a long-distance affair. The three of us live on two continents and in three different cities. Most of our exchanges happened by e-mail. But at several crucial points in the process, we met in Colorado, Maryland, and North Carolina. The times that we were together were some of the richest and most profound discussions we have ever enjoyed. During the course of the writing, we saw an amazing unity of thought emerge among us. Although we had some minor and easily resolved disagreements, we never once experienced a severe conflict. So, while this book is a product of a relationship, it is also true that our relationships with one another have been deepened by this book.

For us, the truths described in this book are not just theoretical or academic. Everything we have written has been foundational in our marriages, with our children, and with our friends. We are far from perfect, of course, but we have seen personally how beautiful life can be when we align our lives with what God has revealed about relationships. Beyond our roles as husbands and fathers, the three of us have almost a century of combined experience working with people around the globe. And we have found that the scriptural principles discussed in these pages are not only relevant but also foundational for good relationships in every culture.

Glenn McMahan
Londrina, PR, Brazil
December 2007

INTRODUCTION

In 1985, Talking Heads released a song called "Road to Nowhere." Although the title sounds pessimistic, the music pumps you up and makes you feel like the ride to nowhere would be a great experience. The giddy spirit of the music makes its bleak meaning seem cool. By embedding a philosophy of meaninglessness in a blissful beat, the song captures the essence of a culture that thrives on momentary, self-oriented pleasures. And that's the way most of my friends and I (Glenn) lived during our late teens and early twenties: having fun, feeling good, but clueless and careless about where we were going. As I pursued one form of emotional stimulation after another, the "Road to Nowhere" was the de facto anthem of my early life. The amusing road to nowhere was my road.

It was difficult to take the big questions about meaning seriously when my life was saturated with entertainment. It was easier to keep the fun marching along, to keep my life busy, and to seek external means of finding temporary joy. But underneath the fun and games I experienced a nagging desire, deep and profound, for something more. I couldn't fully describe the desire nor identify what would satisfy it. But I ached. Inside, I was empty.

The deepest human needs are recognized most when those needs aren't met and the artificial substitutes fail to fill the void, similar to the way strong hunger pangs make us aware of our need for food. Sometimes it takes a dramatic crisis to jolt our souls back to life.

I first felt that hunger when I was sixteen and my parents, who had always provided a peaceful, caring home, announced their divorce. We learned that Dad would keep the house and Mom would take the furniture. After school one afternoon, I walked up the sidewalk, opened the front door, and found nothing inside except the wall-to-wall shag carpet. I sat alone on the living room floor for a while as the sun set and the room darkened. I knew my parents loved me, but I felt as empty as the house.

Three years later, I had another encounter with that hollow ache. I had spent those three years drinking my way into a group of friends. Binge drinking was the only requirement to be in that club. At the time, superficiality and frequent hangovers seemed better than exclusion. My perspective began to change, however, when I went to a friend's house one day at three in the afternoon. His alcoholic mother was just waking up, disheveled and reeking. An argument ensued between them that escalated to a brawl. As mother and son traded punches (the fight didn't last long), that familiar hollow feeling gripped my soul. It was as if I could see my future, and I didn't like what I saw. I knew I needed a different road.

The door to a brighter future opened in a strange way. I had been bar-hopping with a friend who had churchgoing parents. They compelled him to attend services one Sunday, on Easter, I think. He invited me to help him pull through the ordeal. Nothing significant happened at church, but afterward he and I started to talk about the Bible. The more often we talked, the more I read. As I saw the meaning offered by God, I began to see just how bleak the road to nowhere was. The road to *somewhere* became irresistible.

What I had been reading in the Bible became more tangi-

ble through a new group of friends who invested in my life—
people who over the years exposed me to the intellectual riches
of the Bible and showed me a personal God who was interested
in me. As my world opened, I met people with vibrant and intimate marriages. They gave me hope. That hope became a reality when I met my wife and her family.

After a year-long friendship and then a few months of
dating, I knew that I wanted to marry Michelle. First, I needed
permission from her parents. When I arrived at their home
for a nervous talk, they had dinner waiting. In addition to her
parents, Michelle's brother and twin sisters were sitting at the
table. They all knew what I was going to ask, but it took a while
for me to spit it out. Sitting at the other end of the table, my
wife's mother responded by saying something I'll never forget.

"Glenn," she said with tears in her eyes, "from the moment I
conceived Michelle, I began to pray for the husband she would
one day marry. And I strongly believe you are that man."

Her words flooded my heart with the supernatural mercy
of God. Mercy because I knew my life had been in such disarray. If I was indeed the answer to her prayers, it was only by
God's grace. I felt like a lousy soccer player chosen to play on
the varsity team just because the coach liked me. That moment
solidified the new direction of my life.

In retrospect, it was people who lived out the principles
described in this book that put me on the road to *somewhere*.
And the essence of that somewhere—the fulfillment of meaning—was deeply relational.

I don't want you to think that changing directions was
without potholes and detours. It's true that I longed for the
relational meaning I experience today, but even after that mark-
ing moment with my wife's parents, a selfish, fearful side of
me resisted intimacy. It had been there all along, lurking. My
dating relationships in high school and through my early twen-

ties had the durability of soap bubbles. I initiated relationships enthusiastically but discovered an instinctual reflex away from serious commitment. I looked for ways to relate in "safe zones" without risk of rejection or loss of selfish freedoms. When the initial thrill fizzled, I would dump the girl and, in a distorted way, feel piously melancholy about the loss.

That destructive pattern almost shipwrecked my relationship with Michelle during our engagement. On the night I asked my wife to marry me by a fire in the mountains, I felt excited about spending my life with this intelligent, sensitive, spiritually-mature woman whose love of art and jazz brought so much aesthetic order to my life. Our relationship had developed over time, with solid conversations about our direction in life and a genuine enjoyment of each other. This relationship wasn't based on emotional froth like so many of the others. I put the engagement ring on her finger on a clear winter night, motivated by love as fresh as the wind blowing through the mountain pines around us.

But by breakfast the next morning, my heart had turned stone cold. I woke up feeling vaguely worried. As we mingled with friends and announced our engagement, a low-grade angst radiated through my heart. I couldn't identify the source. For no apparent reason the organic joy of the previous night had disappeared. It was like a stock-market crash of the emotions: I was basking in wealth one day and was an impoverished bum the next. Through the weekend I found it difficult to hold her hand, to put my arm around her, or to kiss her.

Days turned into weeks. Confusion and anguish swept over her soul as my stiff communication persisted. Her questions turned to tears when my feeble explanations revealed nothing but an abysmal disconnection between what I knew was right and what I felt. She felt rejected and nearly returned the engagement ring.

I became aware of an alarming paradox. On the one hand, I desperately needed love and intimacy, secure relationships, and the purpose in life that comes from caring for others. But serious flaws lurked below the surface of my character. Selfishness made lifelong commitment to Michelle seem dangerous, because I would have to serve her and not just my personal whims. My vanity created elaborate facades to disguise my flaws. My tenacious pride refused to admit wrong. These traits in my nature, if they had been left untended, would have ended my engagement, and I would have lost the most important person in my life. I would have stepped out of God's meaningful design for life.

I didn't understand the principles of this book at the time, but our relationship survived that early storm because I was surrounded by people who lived according to the truths we've displayed in the following pages. All these relationships, including those with several men who taught me how to proceed, forced me to recognize the flaws in my character. I could no longer hide behind self-protective rationalizations.

The restoration of our engagement sprouted primarily from my wife's willingness to love and forgive me even after I had caused her so much strife. She gave me a safe environment in which I could be honest about my character flaws and still be accepted. She didn't quit.

Ultimately, it came down to a simple decision on my part to do what was right. I knew that loving her was the right thing and that to love her meant changing my behavior. It required me to stop being selfish. As I began to act according to what was right, my feelings for her began to flourish again.

I'll never forget the hours after our wedding ceremony. A light snow had dusted the Colorado foothills. Hand-in-hand we walked on icy ground to the car, supporting one another. I felt a profound sense of rightness. I was certain about the woman

I had just married. She was right. I had a conviction that our love for one another would never be called into question, no matter the circumstances. Beyond all that, however, was the awareness that I was aligned with the way the world was meant to be. Twenty-one years and two kids later, it has been a beautiful road.

My history is evidence that God can give us a meaningful life, despite all our fears and selfishness. And a meaningful life, as we will see, is all about relationships.

Our greatest desire is that this book would help you move toward God's relational design for life. We believe that the principles described in the following pages, which are characteristics of God's nature, can transform any relationship. In fact, your relationships don't have a chance of thriving without the principles described in this book. That might sound like a bold statement, but we say it with confidence. The principles outlined in this book are found in the character and life of Jesus. In following him we find the essentials for relational wholeness.

Most books about relationships focus on a specific problem within an isolated type of relationship. There are books about dealing with strong-willed adolescents, husbands addicted to pornography, post-divorce stress, toddler tantrums, anger, and sexual abuse, to mention just a few. These are usually helpful. But the abundance of specialized books can make us as readers feel like we are attempting to build a three thousand piece jigsaw puzzle without having the whole picture on the box top to guide our efforts.

This book is different. It is intended to help you step back from the isolated, specific issues of the complex puzzle and show you the big picture. We hope to provide you with an overarching understanding of what God designed for humanity, a reflection on God's relational nature.

Therefore, the principles in this book have profound implications for every type of relationship—between husband and wife, parent and child, boss and employee, neighbor and neighbor, teacher and student. These principles are universal at home, at work, and even between nations.

As a result, the universal nature of what Jesus modeled and taught greatly simplifies the plethora of specialized books about hundreds of relational subtopics. In this book we intend to provide what we see as the universal principles of relational wholeness as revealed through God's interaction with mankind. We believe that this framework, illustrated in the life of Jesus, will help you grow in your pursuit of relational wholeness.

QUESTIONS FOR DISCUSSION

1. After reading this introduction, what are your expectations for this book?
2. Are there similarities between Glenn's experiences and your own?

Chapter 1

HUMANKIND'S RELENTLESS LONGING FOR RELATIONAL WHOLENESS

A piercing scream down the long hall of the daycare center sent everyone scrambling. When I (Glenn) arrived at the scene, worried that one of the fifty children who played there after school had been hurt, I saw a boy squatting in a corner slapping his own face and trying to pull out his hair. He had to be restrained for several minutes until he calmed down. Then he wept.

I hadn't known the boy long, and that was my first encounter with his storm-swept soul. It erupted on other occasions during the months that I worked at the center. Even a small conflict with another child would unleash a latent rage. The outbursts kept everyone around him on edge.

I learned that in his brief seven years of life, he had been passed through the hands of seven different foster parents—one destabilizing life-change for every year of his life. Home, family, and school had been repeatedly swept aside and replaced. Continual abandonment had taught him that permanent, unconditional love didn't exist.

Underneath this message churned a growing self-hatred built on the false logic that he was not loved because he was not *worthy* of love. Every time he moved to a new home, the roots of this sank deeper into his mind, further forging a false self-image. Having no reference points to validate his immeasurable value as a person, he came to despise himself.

Six months before I met the boy, a determined and hard-working single woman had adopted him permanently. She told me that she would never desert the boy no matter how difficult the situation became. The boy knew it was a permanent adoption and not just another foster home, but his explosive anger continued. After so many bad experiences, he still found it difficult to trust the authenticity of her love. She believed that she could gradually win his trust and that, as a result, he would recognize his worth.

I admired her courage to assume responsibility for a troubled child with such a complicated past. This young mother would receive no compensation or awards for her valor. But her decision gave hope to an eternal, unique person created by God. She opened the way for him to reach the full potential of his God-given design.

The mother's love couldn't guarantee a positive outcome. Eventually, every child, adopted or not, reaches an age where he must make his own decisions and face the consequences. It's possible that the mother's best efforts would be undermined by the boy's free will. But without her love, the story would almost *certainly* have had a sad ending.

Assuming that the boy matured into a man of character, the mother's decision to serve her adopted son could have a ripple effect that would impact people over the next generations. If the boy becomes a good husband and father, he will edify his family in a way that enables his children to build their own solid families. And so on.

Even if the mother's investment had no broader impact than just on that one boy, the value of her loving decision was immense. When we consider the immeasurable worth of every person, it becomes clear what a valuable contribution she made to the world.

A person's legacy is measured by how well each of us has loved those around us. The apostle Paul wrote, "If I have a faith that can move mountains, but have not love, *I am nothing*."[1] Our life's meaning hangs on the truth of these words.

If only love were simple. But it usually demands that we surmount our selfishness and the fear of rejection. The woman's decision required her to risk her own well-being. She would face emotional stress, financial demands, less freedom, and perhaps fewer chances of marrying. She must have known that her investment would not guarantee a positive outcome in the boy's life or in their relationship. Nevertheless, she believed the personal risk and sacrifice was worthwhile. In light of all this, her decision seems miraculous.

This story demonstrates the fragile, delicate nature of our lives. It may be hard to admit it, but like the boy, we are breakable, dependent, needy beings. Without much effort, we can hurt one another deeply. It doesn't take much to make us angry, envious, or bitter. There is only a fine line in human relations between harmony and dissension. Good friendships can be lost over a simple miscommunication. In this tenuous situation, our lives depend on our willingness and capacity to persistently love one another. It's an inescapable, sobering reality.

Glenn Tinder, in his book *Against Fate*, captures the delicate nature of a person. He says that each individual is a destiny. And by that he means that God has made each of us to be a story in progress, an unfinished work.[2] God influences these stories, and he calls us to live in unity with him and with others. But he doesn't control us. Every person is free and *responsible* (able to respond) to God's manifest desire for our lives. The way our individual stories unfold depends, in part, on how each of us responds to him.

Therefore, because of God's design and influence, we have incredible potential and meaning. But the outcome is not pre-established. A person's story can end in tragedy, triumph, or never be finished. The crux of each person's life—all six billion of us—is relational. That's the way God designed the world.

THE INSATIABLE LONGING
FOR RELATIONSHIPS

It is crucial to understand that our nature is inescapably relational. Even though we are delicate "stories in progress," God has stamped us with the likeness of his own relational nature. This central element of our identity can be suppressed, but it would be like trying to hold your breath; eventually you would turn blue. Any attempt to retreat from relationships will leave us feeling empty and incomplete. To settle for artificial substitutes can never satisfy our deepest needs.

And yet the culture in which we live has become increasingly impersonal. For the last several centuries there has been a dramatic shift in the way we think about the world. New ideas have created doubt about the existence of a personal, relational God. As people have adopted these pervasive ways of thinking and have pushed God to the fringes of life, there has been a corresponding increase in self-interest that has eclipsed God's original, relational blueprint for life.

As a result, relationships today have become more tenuous. We are increasingly fearful of commitment and quicker to bail out under pressure. But humanity's relational nature refuses to subside; people long for intimacy and acceptance.

If you look carefully, you will find this insatiable longing everywhere, sprouting like a desert flower from our arid times. It emerges despite today's brokenness, wars, divorce statistics, and homelessness. Evidence of the relational longing is there, entangled with all the bad news on the front page of the morning paper. But you have to read between the lines to see it.

Our changing views about work serve as one example of humankind's insatiable desire for relational meaning. From the beginning of the Industrial Revolution two centuries ago, mankind has been turned into a means of production, and work has become little more than a way to sustain consumerism. Now people are beginning to question that notion. Is it worthwhile, many are asking, to work seventy hours a week? Where is the balance between work and family? How can we make the office more personal and relational? What can be done to modify the bottom-line mentality and give greater consideration to relational needs?

Former Secretary of Labor Robert Reich told a story in his book *The Future of Success* about how he decided to leave his high-status, highly demanding career in public service. Work became so all-consuming that "all other parts of [his] life shriveled into a dried raisin." One day his youngest son asked Reich to wake him up when he returned home from work late at night, no matter the hour. He had been working so much that the boy just wanted to make sure his father still came home. That short conversation, like a lightning bolt, led Reich to resign. He concluded the book's introduction with a thought that expresses the mindset of many people today. "We can affirm that our life's worth isn't synonymous with our net worth; that the quality of our society is different from our gross national product," he wrote. "We can alter priorities suddenly jolted in the face of mass tragedy, such as a terrorist assault, and acknowledge that relationships with family, friends, and community give life its core meaning."[3] Reich admitted that, due to financial limitations, many people are not able to make the decision he made. Nevertheless, the culture longs for a more relational lifestyle.

Other authors perceive the same worrisome tension. In his book *My Job, My Self*, Al Gini wrote about the "failure of work" to sustain humanity's deepest relational needs: "In a setting where individual workers must constantly compete with the system, themselves and fellow workers, a genuine sense of community cannot and will not occur."[4]

People are looking for ways to recover the relational soul of work. "What employers have asked employees to do since the time of the assembly plants, when Ford first started, was to check their humanity at the door and come in as automatons and just do their work," said author Douglas Noll. "That doesn't work any more."[5]

Beyond attempts to make on-the-job hours more relational and personal, many people have reordered priorities, giving more time to family and community. Gini cites a 1997 *Time* magazine report about the millions of people who are exchanging the impersonal large cities for rural areas. "They believe," says Gini, "that in rural America they won't get lost. They'll become a part of a community where people actually know their neighbors and maybe even make a difference and leave a mark."[6]

Changes like these are not easy for most people. They force people to live in tension with a society built on foundations that put family and community in second place. Life has changed dramatically since the pre-industrial age when the household economy was a family affair. Life wasn't easy back then, but at least the family was together. Fathers had more time and opportunity to teach children about life as they worked together. For mothers, work and raising children happened in a unified way. But the Industrial Revolution and the mass movement from farms to cities fragmented families, forcing parents to work outside the home, distant from their children and spouses.

This happened to my (Glenn's) great-grandfather, who worked as a tenant cotton farmer in Texas before a daughter's illness forced him to move his family to a city in Colorado. My grandfather, who was sixteen at the time, remembers leaving everything he knew behind. He told me before he died at age ninety-seven that it was like "moving to the moon." What he remembers most was that he spent far less time with his father, who worked long hours in a steel mill and came home too exhausted to play.

This growing tendency to question the balance between work and relationships shows up in the film *About Schmidt*. It portrays a retired man, played by Jack Nicholson, who has devoted his life to an insurance company. After the retirement party, he faces the emptiness of his impersonal life. His family relationships have dried up. Then his wife dies, and all that is left is a recreational vehicle.

At one moment in the film, Warren Schmidt says, "Relatively soon, I will die. Maybe in twenty years, maybe tomorrow, it doesn't matter. Once I am dead and everyone who knew me dies too, it will be as though I never existed. What difference has my life made to anyone? None that I can think of. None at all."[7]

In perhaps the most powerful scene, at the end of the film, he is sitting alone at his desk with a picture and letter from a poor boy in Africa, the boy he had "adopted" through a relief organization. This is the only relationship he has left. He reads the endearing letter and weeps, longing for intimacy and relational wholeness.

This longing saturates the film and book industry. Even atheist authors—who believe that the universe is pointless and impersonal—can't escape the tenacious need for personal relationships. In the film *Contact*, based on the novel by the deceased cosmologist Carl Sagan, actress Jodi Foster plays the role of an astronomer who finds extraterrestrial life. Foster's character, Ellie Arroway, is chosen to visit the aliens. Amazingly, the aliens created by Sagan turn out to be personal creatures, despite his belief in an impersonal universe.

"You're an interesting species," the alien tells Ellie. "An interesting mix. You're capable of such beautiful dreams and such horrible nightmares. You feel so lost, so cut off, so alone, only you're not. See, in all our searching, the only thing we've found that makes the emptiness bearable is each other."[8]

In this quote you can hear Sagan's burning need to know that the universe is not a pointless void. Although it contradicts his philosophy of life, you hear his cry for a personal, relational world.

The same longing pumps through the veins of today's youth. Desperate to be accepted, teens will often do whatever it takes to be included in a group. Drugs and alcohol are rites of passage to group acceptance. Gothic dress or certain types of music help them conform to the arbitrary standards of a clique. The molds are always changing, but the basic rule is the same: inclusion at all costs, even if acceptance means denying one's true personality.

"I hung out with punks," said a friend interviewed for this book. "They accepted me, weren't demanding. But real relationships were hard to come by. We practiced serial monogamy. We would stick with someone until it didn't work anymore, then we'd break up. Next time we'd try to 'trade up.' When the lust ended, it was over."[9]

The statistics on youth and family relationships give a mixed bag of results. There are reasons for optimism. Many young people have found safe, good relationships. The divorce rate has been dropping since the early 1980s,[10] and drug and alcohol use among teens has been dropping significantly since the mid-1980s.[11] Most adolescents say they have a good relationship with their parents.[12] Although the relational landscape is still beleaguered, it's possible that these improved trends are an indication of a pendulum swing away from the high rates of family breakdown in the sixties and seventies—perhaps because the consequences have been so painful.

Ethan Watters in his book *Urban Tribes* describes how the generation born in the sixties and seventies has attempted to cope with the high rates of divorce during those decades:

> We all understood . . . that it was our [parents'] genera-tion that had pioneered the record-setting divorce rates and that they were no strangers to the siren song of drugs, adultery, and other forms of self-destructive behavior. Every one of us had, during our adolescence, known an adult who was more confused and in need of guidance than we were at the time. The general social upheaval of the sixties and seventies left them with no solid front from which to attack [us] with advice. . . . The idea that we would let their advice influence our personal choices was laughable.[13]

With family no longer serving as the relational hub, Watters says he and his friends, in "facing the challenge of lives navi-gated without signposts . . . were making up answers—riffing them—as we went along."[14] Divorce became so common that it seemed normal, said Watters. "It would be hard, after all, to realize that your life was off track if everybody in your frame of reference was similarly derailed."[15]

But, amazingly, Watters shows how the longing for whole relationships would not subside—even when there were so few relational reference points. People of that generation substituted the meaningful relationships they lacked at home with what Watters calls the "urban tribe," a loose network of people who concern themselves with one another's well-being. They invented a new relational structure.[16] The urban tribe has become a surrogate family.

In all these cultural trends, we find evidence that regardless of how broken society becomes, mankind's core human trait—the longing for relational meaning—refuses to surrender. One way or another, people will seek ways to satisfy their inherent relational needs.

Why do our souls thirst for intimacy? The Scriptures say that we need relational wholeness because we were created by a relational God. We will take a closer look at the relational nature of God in the next chapter.

QUESTIONS FOR DISCUSSION

1. In this chapter, the authors state that relationships are central to a meaningful life. Do you agree? Disagree? Explain your answer.
2. What other choices (other than relationships) do people commonly make that occupy this central place?
3. Do you experience tension over the competing demands between some of these other choices and relationships? Describe this tension.

4. What are some of the implications for people who choose relationships as their primary value? How would that affect their lives?
5. Do you find yourself desiring intimacy at times and resisting it at other times? If so, when do you notice the resistance and what do you notice about it?

THE DIVINE ROOTS
OF HUMANITY'S
RELATIONAL NATURE

R ecently my wife and I (Glenn) had the rare opportunity to
spend several days without our kids, so we drove to Santa
Fe, New Mexico, to browse the art galleries and museums of
this beautiful southwestern town. The galleries provided refuge
from the cold wind and a feast for the eyes.

In one gallery, we encountered the work of artist Sherry
Karver. She begins with traditional black and white photo-
graphs, transforms them into digital images, and then enlarges
them to enormous sizes. Finally, Karver uses oil paint to bring
about an explosion of color. In the series we saw, she used this
mixed-media method to make compelling images of crowds
walking through Grand Central Station in New York.

The people in the paintings are slightly blurred and ghost-
like. Inside a few of these human forms, Karver imbedded text
that depicts the private thoughts, dreams, hopes, and anxi-
eties of people bustling through a rushed, impersonal place.

The people press toward the next item on the day's agenda, but each is terribly alone. In this way she exposes the tragic irony of how everything meaningful to a person can be trapped inside a private mental and emotional world, isolated from the hurried masses. She captures the grief of anonymity and the paradox of being lonely in a crowd.

Our deepest longings, as Sherry Karver's work demonstrates so beautifully, indicate that we were made for far more than transient and superficial relationships. We should understand that these longings are the heart's cry for a purposeful life centered on relationships. That we long for more is the soul's admission that our man-made culture has failed to provide what we most need. Our longing testifies that something is missing.

Where should we turn?

The heart's longing for a personal and relationally meaningful world helped guide Cambridge University professor and author C. S. Lewis to that ultimate, transcendent answer. It was one of the factors that led him to belief in God. He was an atheist until age thirty-one, but this impersonal perspective couldn't account for his undeniably personal nature. How was it that an impersonal, accidental process could produce such personal human beings? Atheism provided no answer.

As an atheist he believed the world had no inherent meaning, that life was ultimately pointless. But at the same time, he longed for meaning and intimacy. Therefore, he couldn't find any coherence between his philosophy and his deepest longings. In order to maintain his intellectual position, he had to suppress the call of his heart and soul. To satisfy his personal nature he had to live in contradiction with his atheistic philosophy. He was a divided man.

He wrote in *The Weight of Glory* that his deepest longings clearly pointed to the existence of a personal, relational Creator:

A man's physical hunger does not prove that that man will get any bread; he may die of starvation on a raft in the Atlantic. But surely a man's hunger does prove that he comes of a race which repairs its body by eating, and inhabits a world where eatable substances exist. In the same way, though I do not believe (I wish I did) that my desire for Paradise proves that I shall enjoy it, I think it a pretty good indication that such a thing exists and that some men will. A man may love a woman and not win her; but it would be very odd if the phenomenon called 'falling in love' occurred in a sexless world.[1]

Lewis knew the direct connection between the nature of something and its source. Although we don't often think about it, we instinctively look for this same connection between a created thing and its creator all the time.

For example, if you look carefully at a painting in a museum, you will look for and find expressions of the artist's personality, emotions, and perspectives in the painting. You might not be sure of your interpretations, but your impressions won't be totally inaccurate either. If you were able to read something about the artist's life, the connection between the art and the artist would become easier to comprehend. And if you were able to actually talk to the artist and find out what was happening in his heart or mind at the time of the painting, you would have an even clearer understanding of the painting.

Now, bring this analogy to bear on your identity. Imagine yourself as a painting, an original work by an artist who had a purpose in mind prior to your creation. You would expect to find resemblances of the creator in your nature. Now consider the brush strokes of human nature: a longing for intimacy and love, a desire for meaning and purpose, a thirst for eternity, a creative spirit, a resonance with all things beautiful, a moral conscience. What do all these highly personal brush strokes indicate? If we accept the obvious truth that there is a direct relationship between the creator and the creature, then it follows that there is a personal, relational God.

The difference between humans and a painting is that humans are not inanimate paint on a canvas. We are living beings with the ability to make free choices. This amazing freedom, although limited, is yet another of God's brush strokes on human nature. It is a necessary element of human dignity, giving us the responsibility to choose between right and wrong. In fact, human freedom is the necessary ingredient to make sincere and loving relationships possible. Without it, any interaction between people would be robotic and preprogrammed. True love can only exist when people are free to *choose* to love one another.

Therefore, the brush stroke of human freedom enables beauty to emerge from relationships. But it also carries a risk: It means that people can flourish or decay, depending on each person's decisions and life experiences. It means that we can hurt and reject one another. We can miss or even reject the life God wants for his creatures. When that happens, we call it *tragedy*.

There are many theories about human nature that attempt to explain mankind's personal traits without accepting a personal origin. But start with an infinite, relational God, and it's not only reasonable to encounter human nature as described above, it's *predictable*.

To really understand the relational meaning of our lives and to improve the quality of our relationships, the logical first step is to pursue a deeper understanding of the Creator. The more we understand God, the more we can make sense of ourselves and our purposes in life. When we allow God to be the reference point for our relationships, a spectacular, hopeful horizon comes into view.

THE SPECTACULAR TRINITY

What do we mean when we say God is relational? What is our basis for saying that? Jesus provided a glimpse. On one occasion, just before he was arrested, while in prayer to his Father, he said, "Father, I want those you have given me to be with me where I am, and to see my glory, the glory you have given me because you loved me before the creation of the world."[2]

This sentence says that there was a profound, loving relationship even before the creation of time, space, and matter. That's a revolutionary statement. Still more remarkable is that God's purpose was to create people who would experience the same loving relationships and enjoy the same splendor that characterizes God's existence.

But if there's only one God, how could he be relational? It's true that the Scriptures proclaim the existence of just one God, in the singular. As a result, it would be easy to conclude that there was nothing relational about God before he created Adam. But a closer look shows that this singular God is described in the plural. The first chapter of Genesis says, "Let *us* make man in *our* image, in *our* likeness."[3]

In another weighty statement, Jesus gave further definition to the "us" of God. He said, "All that belongs to the Father is mine. That is why I said the Spirit will take from what is mine and make it known to you."[4] Here, one more person is added: the Holy Spirit. Jesus is saying that he, his Father, and the Holy Spirit have all things in common and that they are working together to reveal all the wisdom we need to live well.

The question of how there could be one God made of three persons has been under discussion for centuries. It's no wonder. How does one satisfactorily describe the infinite with finite words and illustrations? Tertullian (c.160–c.225) of North Africa tried to do this by using three words to talk about the triune aspect of God: *persona* (person), *substancia* (substance), and *trinitas* (trinity). He was saying that each of the three *personae*, or individuals, have their place in God's activity and work. Yet the three are of a single *substancia*, an inseparable union distributed in a *trinitas*.[5]

This, of course, challenges our intellectual limits. And it is impossible to fit an infinite God into the box of human thought. But it is helpful to realize that everyday life is filled with metaphors of such a Trinity.

For example, music consists of melody, rhythm, and harmony, yet they make up just one song. The human consists of body, mind, and spirit, yet there is one person. We talk of a universe—*uni-verse*—the *uni*ting of an immense *divers*ification into one cosmos. Christians established the first universities in order to pursue diverse and specialized knowledge in a unified, collaborative way. An ideal marriage is a man and woman forming one identity without diluting the distinctness of each person.

Obviously, these are frail attempts to describe an infinite being. However, in the Trinity we find the only true basis for the personal, relational aspects of human nature. Our longings for relationships can be traced back to God's relational character. He is relational, we were created in his image, and therefore we are inherently relational.

It follows, then, that when our relationships with God and one another fail to thrive, we experience an inner dissatisfaction, a longing for more, a sense that life is incomplete, like the isolated figures in Sherry Karver's paintings.

By looking more closely at the Trinity, we can identify the basis for two essential components of all relationships: the value of the *individual* and the value of *community*. These two aspects of God serve as the backbone of all human relationships.

THE VALUE OF THE INDIVIDUAL

First, because every person was created by a personal God and is not the result of an impersonal cosmic accident, humans have the basis for their intrinsic and infinite value. God created us with forethought and purpose. He proclaims our value. Therefore, our worth doesn't depend on physical perfection, IQ, race, gender, job performance, or socioeconomic status. Without this transcendent basis for human dignity, society easily falls prey to neglecting its weakest members in exchange for expedient goals.

Second, in God's existence as three united but distinct persons, we also find the basis for our individuality, the inherent value of each person's unique personality, talents, and qualities. In other words, that God is personal and has created us in his image gives us the foundation for the overall value of humanity. That God exists as a union of three distinct individuals provides the basis for the value of you and your unique personality.

This has huge implications for our relationships with one another. The New Testament provides the analogy of the human body to explain the value of our unique differences.[6] The body is capable of a huge array of actions because it has a diversity of specialized parts. In the same way that we need and enjoy the diverse functions of our physical bodies, God created and values the diversity among individuals. He values *you*. Your unique personality is an expression of a triune God.

The differences between people—race, culture, personality—often become a source of conflict. For example, the intrinsic differences between men and women can create dissension in a marriage. If the husband demands that his wife relate to him like his male friends, or if he fails to love his wife according to her femaleness, there will be conflict and frustration.

In reality, the husband needs his wife's female capabilities and the wife needs her husband's capacities as a male. When both husband and wife set pride aside and learn to appreciate these inborn differences, the couple will experience the benefits. As they tap their unique, God-given resources and invest their personalities for the good of the marriage, both husband and wife will thrive. The differences between us are to be valued, appreciated, and enjoyed.

THE VALUE OF COMMUNITY

If we only have a basis for our value as individuals, society easily falls into anarchy. But the foundation for community, as expressed in the Trinity, is a barrier against radical individualism. The Trinity provides firm ground for the value of *community*.

As we have said, God is made up of three distinct individuals. But none of them is an isolated, self-oriented creature bent on self-preservation and personal freedom. To the contrary, what we see among them is a radical commitment to the relationship itself *so that* God can fulfill his selfless purposes in the world. There is nothing selfish about God. God is free of ego.

All through the New Testament, we see Jesus acting in harmony with the Father. One good example of this is when Jesus, seeing his own death approaching, prayed on the Mount of Olives and, sweating blood, said, "Father, if you are willing, take this cup from me; yet not my will, but yours be done."[7]

Jesus freely surrendered his own individual status, dignity, and physical comfort in order to maintain the harmonious integrity of the Trinity, and, as we will see in the next chapter, in order to reopen a relationship with humankind. The model of Jesus is crucial for us to understand if we are going to counter the radical individualism of our times.

RADICAL INDIVIDUALISM

The roots of individualism run deep in America's history and culture. In the late 1800s, influential poets and writers such as Ralph Waldo Emerson and Walt Whitman gave voice to the already latent cultural desire to destroy all "barriers to the welfare and the expression of the individual."[8]

Emerson wrote an essay called "Self-Reliance," proclaiming that "nothing is at last sacred but the integrity of your own mind."[9] Then he affirms "that a true man belongs to no other time or place, but is the centre of things."[10] He calls for selfish isolation: "At times the whole world seems to be in conspiracy to importune you with emphatic trifles. Friend, client, child, sickness, fear, want, charity, all knock at once at thy closet door, and say,—'Come out unto us.' But keep thy state; come not into their confusion."[11]

Walt Whitman wrote perhaps the most blatantly egotistical poem in history, titled appropriately "Song of Myself." In this culturally influential eulogy to himself and to the deification of the individual—1346 lines long—the reader finds unabashed selfishness:

What is commonest, cheapest, nearest, easiest, is Me.
Me going in for my chances, spending for vast returns,
Adorning myself to bestow myself on the first that will
    take me. (258–260)

. . . .

Divine am I inside and out, and I make holy whatever I
        touch or am touch'd from,
The scent of these arm-pits aroma finer than prayer
This head more than churches, bibles, and all the creeds.
    (524–526)

. . . .

I have said that the soul is not more than the body,
And I have said that the body is not more than the soul,
And nothing, not God, is greater to one than one's self is.
　　(1269–1271)

. . . .

I hear and behold God in every object, yet understand
　　God not in the least,
Nor do I understand who there can be more wonderful
　　than myself. (1281–1282)[12]

These authors try to establish the individual as the final authority and goal of life, thereby undermining the pursuit of relational intimacy, service to others, and sacrifice for a greater good.

For the self-oriented culture, "the only valid contract is one based on negotiation between individuals acting in their own self-interest," wrote the authors of *Habits of the Heart*. "No binding obligations and no wider social understanding justify a relationship. It exists only as the expression of the choices of the free selves who make it up. And should it no longer meet their needs, it must end."[13]

The Trinity stands completely opposed to such radical individualism. The triune nature of God provides the absolute foundation for the infinite value of each individual, but it also defies the deification of the individual. The Trinity provides no basis for making selfish pursuits the highest reason for existence.

Based on the Trinity's expression of community, we conclude that our lives will only be fulfilled when our relationships have an importance that is greater than a life of self-oriented pursuits.

OUR HIGHEST CALLING

As amazing as it might seem, Jesus made it clear that he hopes all people will experience a relational life that is as profound as the eternal relationship he has with the Father. Not long before he died, Jesus revealed this desire in a prayer:

> I pray also for those who will believe in me through their message, that all of them may be one, Father, *just as you are in me and I am in you*. May they also be in us so that the world may believe that you have sent me. I have given them the glory that you gave me, *that they may be one as we are one*: I in them and you in me. May they be brought to *complete unity* to let the world know that you sent me and have loved them even as you have loved me.[14]

When we think about how to define whole relationships, God himself is our reference point. The relationship within the Trinity is what God wants for us in our relationship with him and with one another. We should not look to cultural trends as the object of our desire. Otherwise we risk living like the figures in Sherry Karver's paintings.

As we will see in the next chapter, God, motivated purely by his relational heart and love for us, has done everything possible to seek us out and call us to himself.

QUESTIONS FOR DISCUSSION

1. What, according to the authors, is the origin of the human longing for relationships?
2. What defines the value of the human being?

3. How does our culture answer this question regarding the value of the individual? According to our popular notions, what defines a person's value?

4. What evidences do you see in our culture of the radical individualism the authors describe?

5. Ultimately, what are the effects of such individualism
   • on the individual?
   • on society?

6. How does this individualism correspond with God's ultimate purpose for mankind?

Chapter 3

EXPRESSIONS OF GOD'S RELATIONAL HEART

O ne of the most perplexing questions people ask about life
is why God created the world in the first place. And every
person arrives at a point in life when he wonders why he exists.
These are difficult questions to answer, so we often avoid them.
But they lurk under the busyness of life. We can't help wondering what might have motivated God to create the world and
then bring us, as individuals, into it.

Some believe that God created humans because he was
lonely and needed companionship. They perceive God as a
solitary old man who created us to satisfy his unmet relational
needs, as if God needed a lap dog to keep him company. They
imagine that God was sulking in the heavens, frustrated and
perhaps depressed prior to our creation.

But, as we saw in the last chapter, the Scriptures say that God
is an eternal, relationally perfect bond of three distinct persons.
Therefore, God did not need to create people to satisfy an

unmet need; he *had* no needs! To the contrary, in the Scriptures we find a God so full of joy, love, and beauty that he's unable to contain it.

It is our view that God created the universe and us to share his bounty with beings capable of receiving and revering all that he gives. His motivation was pure, endless generosity. His perfect and abundant relationship in the Trinity was so beautiful that it had to be shared.

If you look carefully, you will be able to see God's generous and relational heart spilling over through history. God has pursued a relationship with humankind from the moment of creation to the formation of his people in Israel to the coming of Jesus to the spread of his Word to all corners of the earth, and even into our individual hearts. He has cut a path from the cosmos to us. At every level we see traces of his relational heart.

OUR PERSONAL UNIVERSE

God has been trying to convey his love for us since the beginning of time, and often with a very loud voice. King David penned the lines:

The heavens declare the glory of God;
    the skies proclaim the work of his hands.
Day after day they pour forth speech;
    night after night they display knowledge.
There is no speech or language
    where their voice is not heard.
Their voice goes out into all the earth,
    their words to the ends of the world.[1]

Today city lights and urban life have disconnected us from the beauty of the night sky. When I (Glenn) was about ten years old, I went to a ranch in Wyoming, where some friends and I spent a clear and moonless night outdoors without a tent. The only visible light came from the stars. There was a meteor shower that night. Its beauty was so overwhelming that I couldn't sleep. My eyes just went back and forth for hours in the crisp silence as I watched the meteors burn and vanish from the backdrop of the Milky Way. God spoke to me that night in a way that marked my life. There was no audible voice, but he touched my soul. I experienced what King David wrote. God spread out the universe as a means of communicating with *us*.

This awesome fact dumbfounded King David. He couldn't fathom how or why God would create such an immense physical reality and still think about such a small creature like him. So he wrote:

> I look up at your macro-skies, dark and enormous,
>   your handmade sky-jewelry,
> Moon and stars mounted in their settings.
>   Then I look at my micro-self and wonder,
> Why do you bother with us?
>   Why take a second look our way?[2]

The vast and perfect universe makes us realize that we are small. But David also recognized that God does "bother with us" and "look our way." His poem expresses the profound realization that God's love for us is fact even though we are small.

I don't often get the chance to witness a meteor shower on a clear Wyoming night, so I like to read books about cosmology and biology. What I read is like the music of Bach. It moves me and brings me joy.

I once read that if the energy at the first moment of creation had been different by one part out of 10^{120} (that's a 10 followed by 120 zeros) there would be no chance of life anywhere in our universe. One astrophysicist, Michael Turner, described this precision "as if one could throw a dart across the entire universe and hit a bull's-eye one millimeter in diameter on the other side."[3] Perhaps I'm odd, but what I see in that precision is God's love for humanity.

I was awestruck by God when I learned that Earth is situated perfectly in a safe region of the Milky Way, far from hazardous active star formation, supernovae, and the giant molecular clouds often found in the arms of our spiral galaxy.[4] I saw the loving heart of God when I read that the presence of 10 billion-trillion stars in the heavens is not a random way to fill space but the perfect number needed for the complex fusion of heavy elements; that our solar system has the exact distribution of large and small planets needed to clear the way for Earth's migration through space; that the sun is a yellow dwarf, a less common type of star that emits the perfect balance of red and blue light to provide for photosynthesis. How could I not see God's relational heart when I read that the moon helps maintain the exact life-sustaining tilt of Earth's axis and that if it were different by even one degree, life would be impossible?[5]

Author Patrick Glynn resonated with my soul when he wrote that many scientists today agree that "all the seemingly arbitrary and unrelated constants in physics have one strange thing in common—these are precisely the values you need if you want to have a universe capable of producing life. . . . The vast, fifteen-billion-year evolution of the universe had apparently been directed toward one goal: *the creation of human life*."[6]

We live and breathe in a majestic, universal cathedral, a place of worship that surrounds us with God's love and provision. To worship nature would be to deny the grand architect of all things, but we should worship *in* nature, every day, at every meal, at every waking moment, at every sunset.

What God is this who went to such extreme lengths to fine-tune an entire universe for such small beings? How can I ever comprehend the immense love and generosity of creation's maestro, the God who speaks to us in the night sky as we fly at 72,000 miles per hour around the sun? And what is wrong with my heart that I could go through so many days forgetting that every magnificent, intricate cell in my body is a gift from God? How can I be thankless when God aligns every life-sustaining light particle/wave perfectly on the spectrum and then pitches them at 300 million meters per second so that farmers can harvest wheat and we can have toast for breakfast? Why, after all this, do we still find it so extraordinary that Jesus turned water into wine?

You might think that the perfection and beauty of the universe would have been sufficient for God. But nature is not the only means God used to make himself known to mankind. He has also engaged himself in human affairs, in history, in ways that make his participation unmistakable.

GOD'S WORK IN HUMAN HISTORY

In about 2100 BC, God spoke to a man, Abraham, and said,

> I will make you into a great nation
>   and I will bless you;
> I will make your name great,
>   and you will be a blessing.
>
> . . . .
>
> and all peoples on earth
>   will be blessed through you.[7]

Over the next 250 years, Abraham's clan slowly inched its way from two to seventy-two. At that point, Abraham's grandson, Isaac's son Jacob (or Israel), together with his twelve sons and their families, migrated to Egypt. Life there started well, but before long the budding clan found itself enslaved. They spent the next 430 years in slavery. It didn't seem like a good start, but God helped them prosper and grow. By about 1450 BC, the Israelites had grown to be a million strong.

Later God called Moses, who was wanted for murder in Egypt, and gave him the task of delivering the Israelites from slavery. With considerable supernatural assistance from God, the Israelites escaped from Egypt. They had very little knowledge, almost no cultural formation, and zero land. Freedom became harder than slavery, and they grumbled. At least in Egypt they had a regular soup line.

Over the next 700 years God transformed them into a nation. He gave them laws: civil, ceremonial, and moral laws—a total of 613—that covered everything from judiciary matters to personal morals, economics, agriculture, social structure, health and hygiene, and worship. Through these words of wisdom, God taught his people about life as a mother teaches her child to look both ways before crossing the street.

God's purpose in working with this group of people was to reveal himself to the entire world. His motive, again, was relational. He wanted to make the whole world flourish through a knowledge of and relationship with him.

Looking at the whole, it's surprising that God would choose a group of slaves to reveal himself to the nations when one would think he would have chosen a powerful empire. But soon the weak kid on the block grabbed the neighbors' attention. Moses explains why such grand wisdom had been given to such an insignificant nation:

This will show your wisdom and understanding to the nations, who will hear about all these decrees and say, "Surely this great nation is a wise and understanding people." What other nation is so great as to have their gods near them the way the LORD our God is near us whenever we pray to him?[8]

God's relational heart longed to see the entire world know him and accept his love. Unable to find a natural explanation for Israel's growth, the world could only conclude that something supernatural was happening.

You can see the relational heart of God even when the Israelites turned away from him. He warned them countless times not to depend on themselves, but more often than not they didn't listen. So God made the tough love choice to give "them over in the sinful desires of their hearts,"[9] to experience the painful consequences of their own decisions, all the while hoping they would return home.

We might cringe at the Old Testament accounts of bloody destruction and think God is awful. But the disasters are mainly self-inflicted, the consequences of a nation's destructive choices. At one point, God warned the people,

Your own conduct and actions
    have brought this upon you.
This is your punishment.
    How bitter it is!
    How it pierces to the heart![10]

God experienced the terrible pain parents feel when a grown child strays from what is good and true.

As is often the case in our own relationships, Israel's story is both tragic and hopeful. The nation was divided, then repeatedly attacked, and finally conquered. But a small number was taken into exile. With this group of people, God continued to reach out through Israel to the nations of the world, as he had promised Abraham.

GOD ON THE GROUND

After all of God's attempts to draw his people into a relationship with him, and after so many hurtful rejections, you would think that God would have given up. Instead he decided to give even more to us. He sent his Son, God himself in human form.

The Jewish people were suffering under the Roman government when Jesus came on the scene. Although they had been through about four hundred years of exile that included several major cultural and political transitions, Roman rule was probably the most oppressive. Jesus didn't do much to help rescue them from the political situation. He had bigger plans for a permanent, transcendent kingdom that would last through all the generations and that would be entirely based on a personal relationship with him.

People usually concentrate on all that Jesus sacrificed. But think about the sacrifice of the *Father* who sent his Son. It couldn't have been easy for the Father to give those marching orders. His thoughts and emotions might have been a mix of joy, love, and pain. Pain, because God knew that the redemption of humanity required a cross and that only God had the spiritual capital to buy humankind out of its self-inflicted slavery. He felt joy and love because this act of limitless generosity would demolish the towering wall of sin and death that divided mankind from God, allowing us to be (fathom this) God's children.

Imagine what the Father might have felt when Jesus, in Gethsemane, asked for a different cup? The father apparently replied, "No, there is no other way." Saying no to Jesus meant that God could keep the door of his house open for us, even though we had decided to live on the streets.

Perhaps the most difficult moment in the story happened when Jesus, breathing his last on the cross, cries out, "My God, my God, why have you forsaken me?"[11] At that point the Father had to distance himself from the Son. Why? Jesus had absorbed the entire load of humanity's sin in order to take it with him to the grave. The Father's holiness could not be in contact with that sin. So he turned away as the Son plunged to the pit. For the first time in all eternity, the Trinity had been fractured.

"Here is the second person of the Trinity, incarnate God, taking my stead, my place," wrote Francis Schaeffer. He went on:

> In my place, the separation that is a result of man's sin is carried into the Trinity itself. Scripture says that at this point the sun was darkened, and there were shakings of the earth. But surely if we understand this not as some religious story but understand it rather as that which is, can we wonder that the earth shakes?[12]

The Scriptures say that Jesus went through all this because of his generous love for us: "For God so loved the world that he gave his one and only Son, that whoever believes in him shall not perish but have eternal life."[13] That old stand-by verse that many kids memorize captures God's motivation: He *loved* the world, so he *gave* his only Son. Love inspired his generosity.

TO THE ENDS OF THE EARTH

Not long after Jesus' death and resurrection, Paul encouraged the small groups of people who had decided to follow Jesus to remember to live according to their identity in Christ. His message was, you are "fellow citizens with God's people and members of God's household . . . being built together to become a dwelling in which God lives. . . . Live a life worthy of the calling you have received."[14]

In other words, Paul reminded them that they were part of the same relational, love-filled story God had been writing through all of history. They were to see themselves as part of that destiny, the same purpose that was first expressed at the moment of creation, the romance that was born out of God's relational heart.

Sociologist Rodney Stark, concluding his book about how the early Christian church managed to rise from a marginal sect to a world-changing movement, made this remarkable observation:

> Christianity *did not* grow because of miracle working in the marketplaces . . . or because Constantine said it should, or even because the martyrs gave it such credibility. It grew because Christians constituted an intense community. . . . I believe that it was the religion's particular doctrines that permitted Christianity to be among the most sweeping and successful revitalization movements in history. And it was the way these doctrines took on actual flesh, the way they directed organizational actions and individual behavior that led to the rise of Christianity.[15]

Stark's thoroughly researched and documented conclusion shows that it was primarily quality of the *relationships* among the early believers that led to the dispersion of their faith in Christ through the first century. The foundation for this remarkable influence was the belief that God loves each person individually, something that the world at that time had rarely considered, said Stark. Based on that radical idea, the early Christians took seriously the command to love one another, first in their families, then in their Christian communities, and then in the society at large. As a result, in the midst of the brutal, iron-fisted Roman culture, "What Christianity gave to its converts was nothing less than their humanity."[16]

Here we are, more than two thousand years later, and the story continues. God's greatest heart-desire hasn't changed since he formed the stars and galaxies, raised up a nation to bless all the others, and entered time and space to die on a cross. He still wants to share the abundance of his relational heart. He is actively pursuing people in a way that is specific and personal to each person.

GOD'S INDIVIDUAL TOUCH

What we want to know from the history of God's work in the world is whether or not he will give personal attention to each of us, today in the twenty-first century, in ways that we can understand. The answer is yes, he is still giving generously, and he continues to call us personally to a relationship with him.

There have been many ways God has done this in my (Glenn's) life. One example was when my first son was born. After a fifty-six-hour labor and a natural delivery, my brave and brilliant wife, Michelle, nursed a ten-pound boy in the soft window light of a hospital room as I made phone calls to family and friends. I tried unsuccessfully to describe to my father-in-law and coauthor of this book, Jim, the intense new love I felt. But he knew what I was trying to say and told me that being a father would deepen my understanding of God's love for us.

"Now you know something of God's love for *his* Son," he said over the phone. "Think about how much you love your son. Now, could you give him over to a cross?"

If God loved his Son as much as we loved ours and then asked him to give up his life for our sake, just imagine how much God loves *us*.

Now I have a second wonderful son. I can't describe the immensity of the love I have for them both. Knowing my love for them, I still think about how amazing is God's generosity and his desire for us to have a relationship with him. God has used the experience of being a father as one means of speaking to me about his profound love, generosity, and relational heart. I have seen him speak to other people, too, always in personal ways.

For some people, like Francis Collins, leader of the Human Genome Project, God worked in quiet ways over the span of his life. In his acclaimed book *The Language of God*, Collins said that he was raised in a family where faith "just wasn't very important." As a child, Collins was "vaguely aware of the concept of God." As he grew, he began to sense a longing for something beyond himself. He was often touched by the beauty of nature and aesthetic experiences with music. But in college most of these experiences were suffocated by pervasive atheistic arguments. As he completed a PhD in physical chemistry at the University of Yale, Collins became increasingly atheistic, believing that "no thinking scientist could seriously entertain the possibility of God without committing some sort of intellectual suicide."[17]

However, God continued to work personally in Collins' life, in surprising ways. As Collins became disillusioned with his career choice of physical chemistry, he took a course in biochemistry that showed him the astounding world of genetics. He decided to change courses and pursued medicine at the University of North Carolina. By his third year, Collins was thrust into the intense world of caring for sick patients in the hospital. God used this unlikely world of death and disease, however, to speak personally to Collins:

I found the relationships that developed with sick and dying patients almost overwhelming. What struck me profoundly about my bedside conversations with these good North Carolina people was the spiritual aspect of what many of them were going through. I witnessed numerous cases of people whose faith provided them with a strong reassurance of ultimate peace, be it in this world or the next, despite terrible suffering that in most instances they had done nothing to bring on themselves. If faith was a psychological crutch, I concluded, it must be a very powerful one. If it was nothing more than a veneer of cultural tradition, why were these people not shaking their fists at God and demanding that their friends and family stop all this talk about a loving and benevolent supernatural power?[18]

God used one patient in particular, an older woman suffering daily from untreatable angina, to personally touch Collins' heart. After many discussions with her about faith, the woman finally asked Collins what he believed. He didn't really know what to say, but finally stammered, "I'm not really sure."[19] The question woke him up to the fact that he had never pursued his worldview with serious, intellectual intent. In fact, he realized that he had been running from the big questions of life.

That led Collins to read everything he could find about the world's religions. In this process, he found the book *Mere Christianity* by C. S. Lewis, in which Lewis (a former atheist) provided strong intellectual reasons for faith in God. After reading this book, Collins "realized that all of my own constructs against the plausibility of faith were those of a schoolboy."[20]

Collins' story depicts how God persistently uses experiences, people, books, beauty, and argumentation—indeed he uses *anything* to speak in personal ways to each individual. He is not limited in his ability to touch each of us according to our individual personalities and situations.

And then there is one of America's best writers, Annie Dillard. She tells a personal story that seems to have been God's way of poking his love into her life. She was a little girl. It was Christmas Eve. A neighbor, Miss White, showed up at the door dressed as Santa Claus. But Dillard ran away.

"Like everyone in his right mind, I feared Santa Claus, thinking he was God," she wrote:

> I was still thoughtless and brute, reactive. I knew right from wrong, but had barely tested the possibility of shaping my own behavior, and then only from fear, and not yet from love. Santa Claus was an old man whom you never saw, but who nevertheless saw you; he knew when you'd been bad or good. He knew when you'd been bad or good! And I had been bad.[21]

Over time Miss White and Dillard developed a friendship. They did finger painting together and ate cookies. But six months after the Santa Claus encounter, Dillard again ran away from her friend. They had been playing with a magnifying glass and Miss White accidentally focused the sunlight to a point on Dillard's hand. It burned. Miss White tried to explain, but Dillard kept running for home.

"Even now I wonder: if I meet God, will he take and hold my bare hand in his, and focus his eye on my palm, and kindle that spot and let me burn?" she wrote, recalling the meaning of that experience:

> But no. It is I who misunderstood everything and let everybody down. Miss White, God, I am sorry I ran from you. I am still running, running from the knowledge,

that eye, that love from which there is no refuge. For you meant only love, and love, and I felt only fear, and pain. So once in Israel love came to us incarnate, stood in the doorway between two worlds, and we were all afraid.[22]

Only you know your story. But we believe that God is calling us all to participate with him in a relational life that extends from the core of his nature, across the cosmos, into history, through the hearts of the early believers and into our daily lives.

The relational way of life is a grand and meaningful adventure, full of risks, victories, losses, pain, and moments of confusion. But it is the *right and good and beautiful path*. It is the road that God has been on for all eternity. Life is about relationships.

God has provided us with some specific guidance and help as we seek to follow his lead in a relational life. As we look at the life and character of Jesus, we find that he set up signposts to guide us along the way—the four essentials of relational wholeness. The next section of this book focuses on those essentials.

QUESTIONS FOR DISCUSSION

1. What, for you, are the most compelling evidences for the existence of a personal God?
2. What can we learn about God
   - by observing the natural world?
   - through the Old Testament record of God's dealings with the Israelites?
   - from the accounts of Jesus' life and death?
3. What do these revelations from God about himself lead us to conclude about what's important in life?

Chapter 4

THE 4 ESSENTIALS OF RELATIONAL WHOLENESS

It was a clear and crisp September day in Colorado, with a sky so blue it was almost black. I (Glenn) hadn't hiked in the mountains for two years, so I drove through Garden of the Gods with its red sandstone spires and then up Highway 24 to the Waldo Canyon loop. It's a seven-mile trail that offers spectacular views of the 14,110-feet high Pikes Peak. I had an MP3 player stocked with Bach, Beethoven, Miles Davis, and the Modern Jazz Quartet. Could there have been a more perfect concert hall?

After about ninety minutes at a quick pace, I reached the trail's summit, descended into a thick forest of pines, and encountered an unmarked bifurcation. It had been so long since my last trek around the loop that I couldn't remember which direction to take. I was not in danger of getting lost, but the sun was setting, and I was ready for an espresso at my favorite café.

Uncertain, I decided to take the wider, more heavily used trail that headed downhill. I began to worry more when, after thirty minutes of walking deeper into the valley, I hadn't found any signposts to confirm or refute my decision. The descent was steep, and I realized that if I didn't find a marker soon, I might have to climb back out of the valley. I stopped and, as Frank Sinatra sang "New York, New York," wondered if I had made a mistake. But I decided to continue in the same direction; it would have been, after all, hard work to hike back to the other trail. Finally, I encountered a trail marker. To my relief it indicated that I had chosen correctly. The preoccupation dissolved, and I was able once again to relish the music, the autumn colors, and a red-orange sunset over the Rocky Mountains.

It's amazing how a little certainty in life can create such peace. But in life, instead of one unmarked bifurcation, we usually face hundreds of crucial decisions and signposts pointing in all different directions. We often arrive at a crossroads with multiple options, but the conflicting markers leave us bewildered and unsettled. We don't know which signs to trust.

When the apostle Paul wrote his letter to the Christians in the city of Ephesus, he singled out four characteristics in which followers of Christ should imitate him in order to find their way through all the conflicting markers in life. He begins by making the point that they, those common, ordinary citizens of Ephesus, were also citizens of God's kingdom. They were already "seated . . . with [Christ] in the heavenly realms."[1]

Okay, you say, but what about now? What about making it through today? If that's who we are and where we're headed, what is life here and now to be about? How are we to live? Most of the letter to the Ephesians addresses this question.

Paul assured them that God provided everything they needed to live up to their lofty new status. The Holy Spirit would be there for them, giving them the strength. From there, most of the rest of the letter addresses the subject of this book: the manner in which people are to relate to one another. He instructed them to *imitate* Christ in his character, specifically in the four areas we are identifying as the essentials of relational wholeness.

Regarding the first essential, he wrote, you are "to be made new in the attitude of your minds; and to put on the new self, *created to be like God in true righteousness and holiness.*"[2] We've used the word *integrity* to summarize this characteristic. It means "wholeness."

A few lines later, Paul went on to identify the second essential, "Be imitators of God . . . and live a life of *love*, just as Christ loved us and gave himself up for us."[3]

Then, as to the third, he said, "Be completely *humble* and gentle."[4] In another letter, Paul expanded this point further: "*Your attitude should be the same as that of Christ Jesus*: Who, being in very nature God . . . made himself nothing, taking the very nature of a servant. . . . He humbled himself and became obedient to death—even death on a cross!"[5]

Finally, he said, "Be kind and compassionate to one another, *forgiving* each other, *just as in Christ* God forgave you."[6]

Of course the Scriptures have much more to say about relationships than just these four essentials. They provide us with guidance about specific relational problems too—everything from raising children to caring for sick friends. But everything specific in Scripture tends to be a subset of the four essentials.

Some people, by the way they relate to others, leave a trail of hurt and pain as they go through life. Others bring healing and joy and health. Which of these two outcomes prevails in our lives depends on the degree to which our character can be defined by the four essentials.

We learn two things about our thesis from these Scriptures. First, God himself is to be our model for each of these characteristics. Taking our cues from people around us or from our culture isn't good enough. We are to live according to our status as citizens of God's kingdom. It means living a counter-culture lifestyle.

Second, we also realize that these four essentials go far deeper than mere how-to. They are character traits that need to be acquired. They could be considered the common denominators of relational wholeness.

God is saying to us: "See that trail that I followed to get to you? It runs both ways! You can follow it back and find yourself in my presence. And what's more, this same trail will also lead you into the kind of relationships you have always yearned for with everyone in your life."

This is one trail no one should ignore.

THE FIRST ESSENTIAL: INTEGRITY

God started relating to humanity with a big voice that brought the universe into existence. Long before the Old and New Testament had been written, humankind could reasonably conclude that someone eternal, powerful, and intelligent had created the world. Paul, writing in Romans 1, said that the overwhelming evidence of creation left people with no excuse for disbelief.

Nature, however, doesn't reveal much more than God's power and divinity. Creation doesn't fully demonstrate the heart of God. So God didn't stop there. He knew that we would need to know more about him in order to live well.

From the beginning of the story, as God made forays into human affairs, people started gaining a more *personal* awareness of him. Sometimes they had tangible experiences of his actions. God started to introduce himself to mankind as the Lord Almighty, the Holy One, the reference point of all reference

THE 4 ESSENTIALS OF RELATIONAL WHOLENESS

points, the North Star by which everything else is measured. The people who met the Lord Almighty often fell face down in the dirt and couldn't speak. Adam hid from him after his rebellion. After direct encounters with God, one guy limped and another's face glowed.[7] It was terrifying to be exposed to such purity.

At the same time, God made it clear that he cared about his chosen people, Israel. He led them out of slavery, provided material blessings, and taught them how to live. But what they first learned about God was that he was the ultimate source of justice, truth, and righteousness. As Abraham once asked, "Will not the Judge of all the earth do right?"[8] The prophet Isaiah wrote, "But the LORD Almighty will be exalted by his justice, and the holy God will show himself holy by his righteousness."[9] The psalmist wrote, "He will judge the world in righteousness and the peoples in his truth."[10] And, again, "Righteousness and justice are the foundation of his throne."[11]

Notice the important conjunction of these related words: *justice, holy, righteousness,* and *truth.* Together they convey the idea that God is unfailingly committed to what is right and true. We've chosen to summarize these traits with the term *integrity.*

God's integrity—the combination of his holiness, justice, truth, and righteousness—provokes two contradictory impulses in us. On the one hand, we see God's beauty and perfection and we long to be better people, more like him, restored. But God's integrity also makes us want to hide in a dark corner. When we encounter God in a sincere way, awareness of his perfection makes us realize our distorted nature.

When it comes to God's justice, we often treat him like soccer fans treat referees. The refs, those brave people who impose justice in stadiums brimming with testosterone, always get a raw deal. At a recent soccer game in Brazil, I (Glenn) saw thousands of men calling a courageous female referee the most

61

beautiful woman on earth after she called a foul against the visiting team. At that moment, she was in their eyes a super-model. Then, in a matter of minutes, after she ruled a foul against the home team, they called her *vaca gorda* (fat cow). We all like justice until the referee calls a foul on us.

Regardless of how God's integrity makes us feel, it is essential to a relationship with him. Imagine a whimsical, unpredictable, constantly changing, unfair god. To trust such a deity would be like marrying a mafia boss, or worse, a Brazilian soccer fan. But because God has consistently demonstrated his commitment to what is true and right, he can be trusted. Likewise, we need to be people of integrity in order to establish trust in our relationships with one another.

THE SECOND ESSENTIAL: LOVE

If God were no more than a magistrate imposing justice and truth, we'd all be trembling like convicted criminals under the high podium of a dark-suited judge. The result between us and God would be total separation. And what would happen to our relationships if *we* only imposed justice on one another? But God, as we have seen, also abounds in love for us. As he acted through history, he increasingly revealed his loving nature.

Moses understood God's love and staked his life on it. As he waited on Mount Sinai for God's laws, the Israelites danced around a gold calf. They forged the idol to escape the demands of God's integrity. (When all else fails, throw out the referee and hire someone else!) With the gold calf they could try to fill their unavoidable spiritual longings on their own terms. Or so they thought. God saw the scene and felt like a man who finds his wife in bed with another woman. He was rightfully sad, angry, and ready to impose justice. He knew that such behavior, if allowed to continue, would wreak havoc in their lives for generations to come. As God prepared to impose firm limits, Moses appealed to his love. And motivated by this love, God acted in mercy. He kept the doors for a relationship open.[12]

Later Moses reminded the Israelites that

> it was because the LORD *loved* you and kept the oath he swore to your forefathers that he brought you out with a mighty hand and redeemed you from the land of slavery, from the power of Pharaoh king of Egypt. Know therefore that the LORD your God is God; he is the faithful God, keeping his covenant of *love* to a thousand generations of those who love him and keep his commands.[13]

Over time, people began to see more and more evidence that God's justice was inseparable from his love. Now the Lord Almighty also reveals that he is a God of love who picks them up out of the muck, cleans them off, and holds them as they weep. He shows us that integrity is essential to relationships, but that without love they would be equally impossible. We are called to love one another as God loved us.

THE THIRD ESSENTIAL: HUMILITY

God cannot act contrary to his character. But justice and love often make competing demands and create a dilemma. How could God preserve justice and at the same time lovingly spare humankind from the consequences of its injustices? Every parent experiences this tension in daily dealings with children. Your eight-year-old has been tormenting his three-year-old sister all day long. And now she is in tears—again. You feel like sending him to time out for a few years, maybe more. You can't let his behavior continue, lest he, as an adult, torment his wife like his sister. But you also love him. There would be nothing left of the relationship if you only meted out punishment. So what do you do? That tension is, on a small scale, similar to the tension God felt with humanity.

God resolved this tension by doing something incomprehensible: He humbled himself. Consider the following words that the apostle Paul penned to a small group of Christ's followers in the city of Philippi:

Your attitude should be the same as that of Christ Jesus:

> Who, being in very nature God,
>   did not consider equality with God something to
>   be grasped,
> but made himself nothing,
>   taking the very nature of a servant,
>   being made in human likeness.
> And being found in appearance as a man,
>   he humbled himself
>   and became obedient to death—even death on a
>   cross![14]

It's typical for people to think that when Jesus humbled himself he became separate from the Father. But in reality Jesus embodied the humble nature of God. You can look through all the religions, and, with the exception of the Christian affirmations, you will not find any mention of a humble god. What Paul wrote in the above verses is unique in world history. It's almost unthinkable that God would be humble. Why would he do such a thing?

Humility defuses conflict and animosity. It opens dialogue and fosters transparency. God's humble approach to mankind in Jesus was a clear statement that he was a safe haven even though humanity had been so mutinous. Jesus didn't abandon the law and justice. Yet by his actions he left no doubt that people could come to God in whatever condition and find his love. In this way, Jesus modeled how humility is an essential component for all human relationships: It opens the door to intimacy.

THE FOURTH ESSENTIAL: FORGIVENESS

As we have seen, God had to remain true to what is holy and right and fair. He could not brush under the rug all the pain and destruction caused by humankind. There had to be a weighty price paid to balance the scales of justice. Imagine if a judge today simply pardoned a murderer without any penalty. It would devalue the life of the victim and the suffering endured by family and friends. But, at the same time, God's love for us compelled him not to impose the demands of the law. His humility ultimately paved the way for him to resolve the core tension between his justice and love. But the price hadn't yet been paid.

He solved the problem once and for all the day Christ died. Rather than require us to fulfill the demands of justice, Jesus took the punishment on himself and set us free. Peter summed this up with these words, "He himself bore our sins in his body on the tree, so that we might die to sins and live for righteousness; by his wounds you have been healed."[15]

This is the model of true forgiveness. In a broken world full of offenses and revenge, intimate relationships would be impossible without it.

THE SIGNIFICANCE OF THE 4 ESSENTIALS

Taken as a whole, the four essentials—integrity, love, humility, and forgiveness—make up the core of God's nature and everything he does. They also define the parameters for all human relationships. If one is missing, relationships won't flourish. They are universal essentials in every time and culture. They apply to the indigenous tribes in the Amazon, to the executives on Wall Street, to a mother raising kids at home, and to diplomats at the United Nations. In a way, they are to relationships what the universal and inescapable natural laws are to the physical world.

Dorothy Sayers, the British writer and colleague of J. R. R. Tolkien, wrote:

> The village that voted the earth was flat doubtless modi-
> fied its own behavior and its system of physics accord-
> ingly, but its vote did not in any way modify the shape of
> the earth. . . . And if earth's shape entails consequences
> for humanity, those consequences will continue to occur,
> whether humanity likes it or not, in conformity with the
> laws of nature.[16]

In other words, there is truth about the world that exists independently of mankind's opinions and theories. Likewise, there are spiritual and relational parameters that exist independently of human speculation. The more we live in accord with these realities, the more harmonious and beautiful life will be. The further we step out of alignment with the way God created the world, the more stressful and painful life will become. We are free to follow a different trail, but we can't escape the painful consequences of such a decision nor will reality conform to our way of thinking.

Rather than being constrictive and rigid, however, God's parameters for relationships allow freedom for personal expression, individual passions, styles of relating, and cultural differences. To the extent that we collaborate with the four essentials, we are free to explore, build, and invent according to our individual personalities. As we trek through life, these essential character traits serve to keep us moving in the right direction, toward healthy relationships.

God revealed the essentials through the initiatives he took to relate to humanity, starting with his integrity, then showing his love, then his humility, and finally, opening the way to total forgiveness and reconciliation. It would not have made sense for him to proceed in a different order. If he had not first revealed himself as the basis for truth and justice, we would have no ultimate way to determine what is right and wrong. In addition to being lost without a compass, we would have no awareness of our own broken condition. Lacking that, the need for forgiveness would make no sense.

On the individual level, however, the order in which God reveals himself to us varies. God doesn't follow the same course in every person's life. Some people are first impacted by an experience of God's love. Other people approach God with questions of truth, seeking answers for the big questions of life. But ultimately all relationships with God and other people will necessarily involve these four characteristics of God's nature.

The fullest demonstration of God's character was Jesus. The author of Hebrews said: "The Son is the radiance of God's glory and the exact representation of his being."[17] In other words, whatever questions we might have about God can be answered by looking at Jesus. He exhibited each of the four essentials as he lived through the tensions and complexities of life. He showed how all four are interdependent and must work together if our relationships are to thrive.

In the next four chapters, we will take a closer look at each of the essentials as Jesus modeled them. Jesus lived a radical life. To follow him along this pathway is not an easy walk in the woods. It's more like an expedition up Mount Everest. But don't lose heart. God promised to keep you alive on the ascent. And the view is magnificent.

QUESTIONS FOR DISCUSSION

1. In this chapter, the authors have identified four essentials to relational wholeness: integrity, love, humility, and forgiveness. Why are they called "essentials"? Consider the following questions:
   - What happens to a relationship where trust is lost?
   - What becomes of a loveless relationship, where there is no concern for the well-being of the other?
   - What happens in a relationship where pride rules, where one party refuses to listen to the other?
   - How can two imperfect people get along in the absence of forgiveness?
2. Are there really only four essentials? What would you add? Are your additions subsets of one of these four, or are they distinct from them?

Chapter 5

INTEGRITY

"In the world of image, truth is beside the point."[1]

I n 1783, prior to becoming the second president of the United
States, John Adams wrote a letter to his daughter, Abigail
(Nabby), about what to look for in a husband:

> Daughter! Get you an honest man for a husband, and
> keep him honest. No matter whether he is rich, provided
> he be independent. Regard the honor and moral charac-
> ter of the man more than all other circumstances. Think
> of no other greatness but that of the soul, no other riches
> but those of the heart. An honest, sensible, humane man,
> above all the littleness of vanity and extravagances of
> imagination, laboring to do good rather than be rich,
> to be useful rather than make a show, living in modest

simplicity clearly within his means and free from debts and obligations, is really the most respectable man in society, makes himself and all about him most happy."[2]

Why, after all, was Adams so concerned that his daughter should marry an honest man "above all the littleness of vanity," who worked at being "useful rather than make a show?" It came down to one word: trust.

Adams understood the relationship between moral character and a man's ability to care for the daughter he loved. And as any father will tell you, handing your treasured daughter into the hands of another man can be terrifying. Adams knew that relationships are built on trust and that Nabby would need a man who aimed to live on the basis of moral truth. Without a husband of integrity, her life would be full of strife.

Our friends Jack and Cindy found out the importance of trust in relationships after several years of marriage. Jack was thirty years old and starting a new business career. A company offered him a job in another state. It looked like a good opportunity to learn and then assume a manager's position. He decided to take the job, even though Cindy had some serious doubts about the character of Jack's soon-to-be mentor. Jack, however, felt confident that the move would open professional doors, so they pressed on despite Cindy's worries. There was some tension between them as a result.

When Jack started working, the extent of his mentor's personal problems became evident. The man was a playboy who loved expensive parties, and the office staff adored his charisma. By contrast, Jack's quiet personality and love of family made it hard for him to include wild parties and womanizing in his definition of fun. He preferred to spend his free time with his wife and kids. As a result, he soon realized that he was not fitting in well with the staff.

As the company had promised, his mentor retired within two years, and Jack assumed the manager's position. He tried to establish his style of leadership in the office, but the staff refused to accept him as the boss. A small number of people in the office conspired to have Jack fired. They filed a bogus lawsuit accusing him of job discrimination against women. The false accusations forced Jack and Cindy to pay a substantial settlement in order to avoid the high cost of a trial. Jack lost his position as manager and had to take a sales position. He was devastated.

"I didn't doubt Jack's character for the lawsuit issue, but I did struggle with him not heeding the warning signs I saw as they came up months before this happened," said Cindy, who at the time had had more experience with the backstabbing corporate environment than Jack. "I could see red flags everywhere. I was just much more intuitive and in-tune to what was happening, whereas Jack was so trusting . . . I had a hard time convincing him that people can be *bad*!"

Jack stayed in sales with the same company. Lies and rumors persisted because of what had happened earlier. "It hurt deeply," said Cindy. "But he never wavered, never spoke out, never became enraged, never fell into self-pity. . . . He just kept going, like a focused race horse that doesn't look to the right or the left."

Eventually, Jack accepted a better position with a different company, but it required them to make another move. This experience increased their dependence on God. They learned that God often uses disaster to sculpt a person. It hurts when the hammer falls, but something beautiful emerges.

Reflecting on those events, Cindy remembers how difficult it was to feel so helpless, especially when she saw that Jack was "walking into a snare and wouldn't listen to my warnings." But by learning to trust in God, they were able to pass through a severe crisis with love rather than division. As things fell apart professionally for Jack, Cindy could have pummeled him with angry accusations for having moved the family to another state despite her warnings. Instead, she trusted God and supported Jack.

What was it about Jack and Cindy's relationship that built this strong mutual trust? The answer lies in the formative dating years. They remember finding in one another a deep commitment to God and his design for life. Cindy didn't see just a handsome, adventurous outdoorsman. She saw in Jack someone whose life and actions demonstrated a commitment to moral truth. He was kind, gentle, and a servant. "I came to know him as a man of deep personal faith. I loved his heart for the Lord and for people," she said.

The integrity in both Jack and Cindy gave them a basis for trust in one another. And as a result of this trust, intimacy could blossom. When the crisis swept into their lives, they could stand firm in their marriage even when there were differences of opinion, mistakes, and severe external pressures. An unshakeable commitment to one another minimized the fear of division even in the middle of conflict. The source of it all, however, was the sincere relationship each had with God.

THE NATURE OF INTEGRITY

When we talk about integrity, we're talking about glue, the stuff that holds the world together. Integrity is a long-term mind-set, a commitment to one's word and what is true. It produces trust. And trust is essential for intimacy. Without integrity all relationships will fray like the ends of an old rope.

The word *integrity* means "wholeness." It means to be complete, lacking nothing, unadulterated, integrated. When we experience this wholeness, it feels like a symphony in the soul.

Everything fits. A deep sense of "rightness" and peace flows through the heart and mind. It feels that way because integrity always involves living a life that is aligned to God's original design for us. It involves more than just speaking one's mind or being honest about one's opinions. It is about more than mere authenticity — being true to oneself. A person of integrity is a person committed to God's truth and virtue that stands independent of personal opinions.

"Integrity," wrote Stephen L. Carter in *The Atlantic Monthly*, "requires three steps: discerning what is right and what is wrong; acting on what you have discerned, even at personal cost; and saying openly that you are acting on your understanding of right and wrong."[3]

That's a good definition of integrity. Carter says that integrity demands two primary traits in a person. First, it requires firm understanding of what's right in God's eyes. That implies taking the time to pursue truth as revealed in the Scriptures and to grow in discernment and wisdom through the complex and difficult experiences of life. Second, integrity stipulates that we have the *willpower* to act according to God's designs for life, even if it requires significant personal sacrifice.

The problem, however, is our tendency to form ideas of what is morally right on a personal, self-referencing basis. When we establish ourselves as the final authority, "moral reflection" becomes an exercise not unlike a dog chasing its tail. As Carter points out, "a man who was raised from birth in a society that preaches racism states his belief in one race's inferiority as a fact, without ever really considering that perhaps this deeply held view is wrong."[4]

Discerning what's right can often be difficult. Life's decisions are not always black and white. But usually the problem is that we lack the *will* to do what's right, especially when right action requires self-sacrifice. It's easier to adapt the truth in order to facilitate a more comfortable set of circumstances.

This tendency to bend moral truth to serve our desires has affected the broader political and social structures of our society, as well as our personal relationships. It's important to recognize the importance of integrity in both spheres.

INTEGRITY IN SOCIETY

A civil, democratic society hinges completely on a trust relationship between those in power and the people they are supposed to serve. When power is wielded only for the benefit of the powerful, when business leaders and politicians put self-interest above God's moral truth, the trust between the leaders and the people breaks down.

As political scientist Glenn Tinder stated about the loss of integrity in public life, "Politics loses its moral structure and purpose, and turns into an affair of group interest and personal ambition."[5]

When the moral structure is lost, the social and economic costs are incalculable. High levels of government corruption cost billions of dollars every year and, worse, thousands of lives.

According to Transparency International, "The effect of corruption on the social fabric of society is the most damaging of all. It undermines people's trust in the political system, in its institutions and its leadership. Frustration and general apathy among a disillusioned public result in a weak civil society."[6]

In March of 2004, as the press revealed a major corruption scandal in Brazil, an honest airport janitor made national news. While fifty-five-year-old Francisco Cavalcante cleaned a bathroom in the Brasilia airport, something he'd done every day for twenty-six years, he found a bag with $10,000 dollars inside. The bag also contained a passport belonging to a Swiss tourist.

This was a lot of money for Cavalcante, who earned only $120 a month. But he handed the money over to the authorities, who in turn located the tourist and returned the money to its rightful owner. Cavalcante's attitude and action inspired the entire nation during a dark time.

"What I did was what everyone should do," said Cavalcante. "If everyone did this Brazil would be a better place. And there's nothing better in life than to come home and sleep with a clear conscience. . . . This is all I want for my family and me."[7]

If only there were more Francisco Cavalcantes in the world. Unfortunately, what seems to predominate in the news is the age-old pattern of adapting moral truth to justify self-interest—the lack of integrity. This tendency in human nature has created unfathomable suffering.

INTEGRITY IN PERSONAL AFFAIRS

Corruption is not limited to the political systems of the world. We often overlook the ways that we undermine trust in our seemingly innocuous daily decisions. Trust is fragile. It's hard to build and easy to break. But it is at the heart of all human interaction.

A car mechanic damages trust when he tells you that you need to spend five hundred dollars for a new clutch and you find out later that it only needed an adjustment. Trust is the primary issue when you sign a medical release allowing a doctor to perform heart surgery. Trust is at stake when you allow your sixteen-year-old daughter to go on a date and the guy picks her up on a Harley-Davidson. Trust is at the center of every human interaction.

Or imagine these scenarios. Do you expect me to marry you when I can't believe a word you say? Do you expect me to be a loyal employee when everyone knows that management has tossed aside qualified, hardworking employees just because of their age? You want me to invest in your company, even after your last fraudulent venture? How supportive can I be of this government if I worry that elected officials aren't telling the truth?

I (David) once took my wife and kids on a vacation to Philadelphia and New York. After a visit to the Liberty Bell, we encountered a man walking toward us with a dollar bill in his hand. I could hear him asking people, "Does anyone have seventy-five cents? I need change to pay for the subway." I dug into my pocket and found three quarters. As he came by, I gave him the three quarters, but he walked off without giving me the dollar! I stood there, stunned, until one of my kids asked, "Dad, did he just take your money?" I was embarrassed.

Even though I had lost only seventy-five cents, that little con sparked distrust in me. As I encountered needy people in both cities, I was afraid to help them for fear of being duped again. The other people on the street were probably honest, but I found it difficult to get past my skepticism. In this way, distrust can spread as a result of only one person's lack of integrity. Integrity is characterized by long-term moral consistency, but distrust has a long-term memory.

We are tempted to lie every day. White lies help us through awkward moments. When a person is late for work because he overslept, it sounds better to say: "I got a business call just as I was leaving the house." People tolerate these little lies up to a point, but the effect they have on our character can be like the slow erosion caused by water dripping on rock; only over time do you notice the damage. We tell lies because we sincerely desire to please others and keep the peace. Sometimes we say things to make others feel better, or to avoid conflict and anger. Although the motives are good, the results are not. Even good-willed dishonesty reduces trust.

As a counselor, I (David) frequently see how damaging lies are to relationships. They can cause division and perpetuate longstanding relational conflicts. For example, a person who has been involved in an extramarital affair might say "I have never really loved you" to the spouse. This is a lie that shocks and surprises the partner. It is not true to their mutual story but rather a form of rationalization that's required to justify the affair. As long as the person is committed to maintaining the lie, no healthy relationship is possible.

In spite of the divisive results of lying, a number of authors have tried to justify the practice. One writer, David Livingstone Smith, believes that people lie, in part, because humans evolved that way. For Smith, to lie is an unavoidable, natural act that helps society function and benefits those who lie.

"The lie is the pillar of social relations," Smith said in a magazine interview. "To tell lies is a tendency as internalized in the human being as the ability to talk and walk. We don't have a choice not to lie."[8]

It's true that lies at first seem to help life flow more smoothly. But Smith fails to mention how they corrode friendships and marriages. This is to say nothing of how lying eats away the inner character of a person—a fact which, in time, becomes self-evident and apparent to everyone.

Try as we might, there is no way to escape the fact that lies misrepresent, and are therefore a form of injustice. Because they are so widely employed and they breed so much distrust, it might be better to argue that the real "pillar of social relations" is our *tolerance* of the lies. It's amazing that we get along at all.

Explicit lies are just one of the ways we undermine trust in our relationships. A more subtle form of lying—the dependence on facades—also increases the distrust between us.

CREATIVE FORMS OF LYING

It's common for people today to be extremely preoccupied with their image. Ever since Adam and Eve discovered their bare condition and felt shame, humankind has clothed itself with facades that promote the self and cover the broken aspects of our lives.

One reason for this might be the fact that we are so saturated by facades in today's media environment. Propaganda soaks our minds in a sea of false images and phony promises. Advertising *seduces* us. Writer Dick Keyes says that advertisers no longer worry about rational persuasion to sell products. The goal, he says, is to convey an image of how people would like to see themselves—beautiful, free, independent, cool, aloof, dignified, strong—and then connect that projected self-image to the product. In its essence, advertising feeds us portraits of what we would like to find in ourselves but in reality lack.

Given that we are so stimulated by advertising images, we often create an "advertisement" of ourselves too—one that projects what we assume others will like and accept. Such facades are a means of self-promotion, and they are not wholly true. To some degree everyone needs a protective layer, and there are times when we need to put our best foot forward. But there is a lurking danger.

"The focus of life is shifted from who I am and what I do to how I can appear, from reality to image. The seductiveness of this drift is that it seems to be an ingenious shortcut to being a whole person," Keyes wrote.[9]

When a person employs such a "shortcut" to integrity, projecting a fictional person like a pop star on stage, soon he realizes that he is lying to himself. He has to embrace the artificiality of a false, external person that is incongruent with the true self. It requires him to live with a "truth" about himself that he knows is a sham. Thus, he becomes a divided person, having separated the inward reality from the external image. To live with such a contradiction saps vitality from the soul.

Naturally, such facades damage relationships. Imagine a man who is dating a woman and she gives him every indication that she is in love with him. In reality, and perhaps unconsciously, she is only motivated by a fear of never finding anyone else who will love her. Her fears are legitimate and understandable, but in many of her attitudes and actions she is pretending to be in love. By acting falsely she has wrongly placed her own concerns above the man's. Her self-interest has taken precedent over truth. As the relationship progresses, the man puts more and more of his life on the line—both emotionally and practically. After investing heavily in the relationship, he begins to see that her heart is not engaged. The facade becomes impossible for her to sustain, and she realizes that she must end the relationship. He's left confused and hurt by deception.

Ernest Becker, a postmodern thinker, believed that "man's fictions are not superfluous creations that could be 'put aside' so that the 'more serious' business of life could continue." For Becker, people must defend the fictional identity they have invented and then "deny its artificiality" knowing all the while that it is, in fact, artificial.[10] In other words, he encourages us to live a lie and believe it's true.

What motivates people to adopt this way of life, usually in an unconscious way, is the allure of self-promotion. Being free to "invent yourself" offers the appealing feel of total freedom—the sensation that I can be whoever I want to be and do whatever I want to do. The goal is to free ourselves from God's moral truth, to free ourselves from human limitations, to deny the broken aspects of human nature so that we can justify the pursuit of selfish desires.

If we accept this assumption, however, it's hard to comprehend how our relationships can survive. How can you entrust your heart to someone if it's impossible to know what's real about them? What if a friend decides to switch identities in order to pursue a different self-interested goal? In short, if everyone is living a lie for the purpose of obtaining selfish goals, then there can be no way for us to trust one another.

The 1999 film, *The Talented Mister Ripley*, portrays this modern plight. Matt Damon plays Tom Ripley, a young man in the 1950s who works as a bathroom attendant. Hoping to be something more, Tom starts pretending to be a student at Princeton. This facade connects him to people in high society, and they accept him into the circle. Enjoying his new life of luxury, he perpetuates the facades, lies, and forgery. Every lie, however, must be defended by inventing bigger and more complicated lies. Eventually everything depends on his ability to sustain the charade. He becomes so committed to the facade that he eventually murders a man in order to uphold his fake identity.

At one point in the film, Tom says something that captures the temptation of our times: "I always thought it'd be better to be a fake somebody than a real nobody."[11]

What makes someone a somebody or a nobody? If we accept God as the ultimate basis for human value, then our worth does not depend on whether we study at Princeton or work as a janitor. We are valuable because God has valued us. In God's world, our value as individuals doesn't depend on performance. That frees us from the need to invent facades. Trusting God for our ultimate worth enables us to grow into the people he has created us to be. The closer we live with our Creator, the one who knows us intimately and loves us anyway, the more we will find our true self.

By contrast, if we reject God as the ultimate basis for our value, we will feel strongly compelled to fabricate it for ourselves by depending on status, appearance, wealth, intelligence, athleticism. However, all of those things are conditional and insufficient as a basis for self-worth. So we resort to facades, putting on a strong face, hiding under a shiny veneer. From that point, as Shakespeare said, "All the world is a stage." And if everyone is nothing more than an actor, how will we find true intimacy and trust?

JESUS: THE PERFECT MAN OF INTEGRITY

Jesus' life was radically different from our cultural trends and attitudes. He was the perfect model of integrity—a person committed to truth, justice, and goodness, even at great cost to himself. His whole aim in life was to speak and act on the basis of moral truth, the truth about his divine identity, the truth about mankind and our world.

It's surprising how little Jesus worried about his image. You would think that Jesus would have done more to attract large crowds—to establish a political campaign with advertising, public relations staff, and market surveys. After all, his greatest hope was for all people to believe in and follow him.

It's true that large crowds gathered around him after he healed some sick people and provided food for five thousand. Were his miracles just a public relations strategy? Definitely not. Most of those people didn't stay around for long. By the sixth chapter of John's gospel, we see Jesus saying things that the majority didn't care to hear. Imagine a presidential candidate saying this to journalists on the campaign trail: "Whoever eats my flesh and drinks my blood remains in me, and I in him. Just as the living Father sent me and I live because of the Father, so the one who feeds on me will live because of me."[12] He said this to a crowd who had eaten the bread and fish he miraculously provided a day earlier.

Jesus was telling them that a full belly would be insufficient for human existence. Given that humans are spiritual beings, the people around him needed spiritual nourishment. And the only way to be fulfilled eternally, he said, was through a relationship with him. And that's the part they didn't want to hear. They enjoyed the free food and health care offered by Jesus, but when it came to submitting their lives to him, almost everyone bolted. As John wrote, "From this time many of his disciples turned back and no longer followed him."[13]

Ironically, his commitment to moral truth riled the religious leaders most of all. That's because they used religion as a facade in the same way that we employ status and wealth. Jesus' life and words exposed the true condition of those who depended on a religious charade to hide a dark underbelly. Jesus was like a scalpel cutting through their self-righteous hypocrisy. On one occasion he told them that they were "white-washed tombs, which look beautiful on the outside but on the inside are full of dead men's bones and everything unclean. In the same way, on the outside you appear to people as righteous but on the inside you are full of hypocrisy and wickedness."[14]

While he rebuked the self-righteous, he warmly accepted those who admitted their moral failures, the people who were honest about their spiritual poverty. Whether they were materially rich or poor didn't make much difference to Jesus. He was interested in each person's heart, and he tried to help people move beyond the charades.

Most of the time, Jesus related to people with this compassionate demeanor. But on at least one occasion he demonstrated his zeal for truth and justice with a whip. He went to the temple and found it being used as a place of commerce. The people were exploiting religion to make a few bucks. The passion for God had been suffocated by the pursuit of money, and this distorted the truth about God's identity. Knowing that this distortion would be an obstacle to faith in God, Jesus cracked the whip on the stone floor, overturned the tables, and drove everyone out. His action is still a warning against those who would use religion to manipulate people for financial gain.

The integrity of Jesus—his commitment to truth and justice—remained firm even during the days leading up to his execution. It's important to remember that he *chose* to go to the cross on our behalf. The Roman and religious authorities only took his life because he surrendered it to them.

It was not an easy decision. Shortly before his arrest, he spoke with the Father and asked for a less painful way to resolve humanity's predicament. "My soul is overwhelmed with sorrow to the point of death," Jesus said in the Garden of Gethsemane. "My Father, if it is possible, may this cup be taken from me." His next words show his commitment to truth and justice: "Yet not as I will, but as you will."[15]

Here Jesus models the core of what it means to be a person of integrity. He submits his own desires and comfort to the higher will of the Father. He remained faithful to truth even at the ultimate personal cost.

After Jesus allowed himself to be arrested, the religious authorities sent him to the Roman authorities to stand trial for crimes he never committed. He met the populist governor, Pilate, and an angry crowd. Pilate asked the mob what crime Jesus had committed. In a stupendous display of circular reasoning, they replied, "If he were not a criminal, we would not have handed him over to you."[16]

Pilate, finding no reason under Roman law to punish Jesus, told them to "judge him by your own law."[17] (Do you hear the relativism in that line? If one "truth" doesn't enable you to obtain your objective, pitch it out and use another one.) The people, however, living under a Roman system of justice, couldn't carry out the execution they desired without Roman approval. Their law had no teeth, so they pressured Pilate to kill him instead.

As is so common today, they bent the truth to justify what was morally wrong.

Jesus and Pilate then had a conversation inside the palace, away from the screaming crowd. Jesus told him the truth about his divine identity. And Pilate said, as a relativist philosopher would say today, "What is truth?"[18]

He had no basis for a charge against Jesus under any law, Roman or religious, but Pilate was under pressure from a mad crowd screaming for an execution. He was afraid of a riot, which would have made his governance look weak in the eyes of Caesar. The pressure to please the crowd and protect his job built, until finally Pilate washed his hands and sent Jesus to a brutal death, all the while knowing that Jesus was innocent.

The contrast between the character of Jesus and that of Pilate in this story is stunning. For Pilate, truth was like soft clay. It could be molded to serve his personal desires and objectives. Truth was secondary in relation to practical demands, political expediency, and his own professional future. For the sake of personal comfort, Pilate chose to abandon all commitment to moral truth. As a result, justice vanished.

Jesus, on the other hand, had life and death at stake, not just his own life, but yours and mine. The outcome of an eternal drama was on the line. He threw aside his personal comfort, his dignity before men, and his popular appeal for the sake of truth. For Jesus, truth was the unshakeable parameter of his life.[19] As a result of his commitment to truth, Jesus paid the price for Pilate's injustice and ours. Through Jesus we are *justified*.

There is a pointed warning in this story for our relativistic times, when "truth" is often considered to be a repulsive word: *There can be no justice among us where God's moral truth is not highly valued.*

THE TENSION OF JUSTICE

How should God respond to mankind's lack of integrity? Jesus took a strong stand for truth and justice. He hated evil and the suffering it causes. The Old Testament prophecies about Jesus state that his kingdom would be based on truth and justice. Doesn't God have the right to hold us accountable for the ways we corrupt the world? Should he just sweep all our dirt under the rug and pretend it never happened? What kind of God would that be, to turn his back and forget everything? Wouldn't that be the greatest act of injustice possible? After all, we demand justice of others when we've been hurt and abused.

God's justice creates a tension. We want the world to be fair, and we become outraged when justice isn't served. At the same time, we fear that God will hold *us* accountable for our own lack of integrity. Part of us hopes that he will just forget about us and walk away. We dread the thought that one day we will stand before the judge.

We know from the life of Jesus that God is fully committed to truth and justice. But we also know from his life that God loves us. If it were not for his love, we wouldn't have a chance. And without love, neither would our relationships.

What are we to do with this tension between justice and love? What should God do? To that subject we turn next.

QUESTIONS FOR DISCUSSION

1. Why is integrity essential to any meaningful relationship?
2. Why do people lie?
3. In what kinds of situations do you find it most difficult to be absolutely honest?

4. Do you think the use of a little white lie is an acceptable solution in an awkward situation?
5. Are there circumstances in which it is appropriate to present a false image of yourself without it being a breach of integrity?
6. Other than lying, what are some common forms of deceit frequently practiced in our culture? What are the consequences?
7. What happens when trust is broken in a relationship? How can it be rebuilt?

Chapter 6

LOVE

We ended the last chapter with a dilemma. Humankind's lack of integrity, which causes so much pain and suffering, places God in a position similar to that of a parent whose son has committed a crime. On the one hand, the law must be respected and justice must be served. But the parent loves the son deeply and can't bear to see him punished. Can you imagine being in that situation with your child? This was God's dilemma in relation to humanity. He experienced a tension between justice and love.

This tension is born from the fact that truth, justice, and love are an amalgam. We see this by the way Jesus defined the essence of moral truth: Love God with all your heart, soul, and mind, and love your neighbor as yourself.[1] According to Jesus, everything right, good, true, and fair is an expression of love. But love also creates a longing to spare from the penalties of the law those who have committed an injustice.

The way God resolved this dilemma is astounding. The apostle John summarized God's solution in a single sentence: "This is love: not that we loved God, but that he loved us and sent his Son *as an atoning sacrifice* for our sins."[2]

The word *atonement* means to unify that which has been fragmented, to restore something broken to a condition of "at oneness." In our case, the fragmentation between us and God was self-imposed. We chose to turn away from God in order to follow our own pursuits. That lack of integrity has resulted in a broken world. But as we encounter the fateful consequences of that prideful path, God has been working to call us back to himself. Jesus was his way of building a road home. His ultimate goal is to reinstate his relationship with mankind, and his motivation is love.

Jesus was committed to both love and justice. He had a firm commitment to God's holy law, as we saw in the last chapter. But his whole mission in life was to save people from the demands of justice, to restore our relationship with God.

We see this two-fold commitment to integrity and love in a short conversation Jesus had with a criminal who was crucified next to him. As the merciless hand of Roman law drained life from his body, the criminal admitted that he deserved his execution. He assumed full responsibility. Flooded with remorse and a longing for eternity, the man looked to Jesus as his only hope and said: "Jesus, remember me when You come in Your kingdom!" And Jesus replies, "Truly I say to you, today you shall *be with Me* in Paradise."[3]

What a simple and profound exchange. That little phrase, *be with me*, says so much. It expresses the relational heart of God, his desire to be unified with each person.

The criminal had done nothing that would deserve an eternal relationship with God. His life was a mess. His only legacy was a trail of destruction. In the world's eyes, he was nothing more than a filthy criminal deserving death. But Jesus saw past the law and into the man's heart. He did not spare him from the demands of the Roman law, but at that very moment, Jesus was paying the price necessary to provide this broken, bleeding, forsaken man with an inheritance, a home, a family, a place to belong.

The love of Jesus did not depend on the man's performance. Jesus showed him unconditional love. This is the most powerful form of love because it doesn't require perfection. In fact, a person can't earn it, no matter how hard he tries. Unconditional love can only be expressed in the form of a gift, independent of the recipient's merit. This love is by nature an expression of *grace*: to be showered with gifts that you never earned.

Grace bothers us. Most of us are thankful when people give us gifts, but there is also a common feeling that we must do something to "return the favor." We don't like the idea of getting something for nothing, and so we feel obligated to compensate the person for their generosity. When you help poor people in Brazil, they often say, *"Deus lhe pague,"* meaning, "God pay you." They say that because they know they are too poor to pay you back. It's hard for them, as it is for us, to accept something for nothing.

Pride underlies this struggle. We prefer the merit system over the gift system because it gives us the right to boast and display our trophies. But grace nullifies pride. No one can boast about something he has been given. The only legitimate response to grace is thankfulness.

Close friends once gave my wife and me (Glenn) a very valuable, life-changing gift. It was an expression of insurmountable generosity and love. We felt overwhelmed with thankfulness and gratitude. But a twinge of prideful guilt surged in my soul because I had done nothing to deserve it and could never have done anything to pay them back. Standing next to the gift with one of them, I said, "You know, I kind of feel guilty for having something so wonderful that I never earned." One of them paused and then said, "If you think you feel guilty now, just wait until you get to heaven!"

His point was clear. I had been trapped in the "I'll pay you back" mode and therefore missed the beauty of pure love and grace. My friend helped me realize (again!) that God's love can never be earned. And his generosity is so immense that it is impossible to repay. All we can do is be thankful.

When love circulates through the veins of our relationships, everyone experiences an inner rest. This is because perfection is no longer the prerequisite to love and acceptance. It is not required to *earn* love. Grace removes the universal fear of rejection and the demand for performance.

Our society aches for this peace and rest. Today, many teenage girls feel overwhelmed with the demand to be beautiful, thin, and perfect. The perfection quotient pushes them to eating disorders and anxiety. Schools are places where judgment pervades relationships. Kids bully, ridicule, and isolate those who, for whatever superficial reason, seem different from the mainstream. Advertising saturates our minds with ideals of perfection that no one can attain. Suicide is often related to feelings of failure, the inability to meet some impossible standard. People need the love—the grace—that Jesus modeled. They need to know they are accepted and valued *as they are*.

For this reason, the apostle John wrote, "There is no fear in love; but perfect love casts out fear, because fear involves punishment."[4] Without "perfect love" in our relationships, fear of rejection steals the quiet from our souls. Fear drives us to work harder, to be more religious, to become more beautiful, and to earn more status. This is an exhausting way of life. Before long, we become spiritually and emotionally anemic.

Love, however, does not nullify integrity. To love someone does not mean that we condone any and all behavior. People must be committed to moral truth in order for relationships to flourish. Truth and love must operate together. When they do, a relationship becomes a safe haven for mutual transparency.

It allows the other to say to you, "I know what's going on. We both know it isn't right, but I still love you. I am still your friend."

To receive this kind of love is one thing, but in order to *live it* we encounter some formidable barriers in our nature. For this reason the love that Jesus modeled is uncommon in our world.

A DEATH ON MOUNT EVEREST

Sir Edmund Hillary, the first mountaineer to reach the summit of Mount Everest recently said these words: "Human life is far more important than just getting to the top of the mountain."[5]

Nearly everyone would agree with that statement. Or would they?

Hillary made this statement to journalists in May 2006 when he heard that about forty climbers bent on reaching the summit of Everest had denied help to a fellow climber who was dying of oxygen deprivation. According to the reports, the climbers all saw the dying man and left him there.

The man who died was thirty-four-year-old David Sharp. He had just made a successful ascent to the top of the 29,035-foot peak. After reaching the summit, he descended about 1,000 feet. Then he apparently ran out of supplemental oxygen tanks. Without oxygen, muscles become severely fatigued. Prolonged oxygen deprivation, as happened in Sharp's case, leads to high-altitude pulmonary or cerebral edema.

"It was wrong if there was a man dying of altitude problems and huddled under a rock, just to lift your hat, say 'good morning' and pass on by," Hillary told reporters. He also said that what happened to Sharp had happened on other expeditions, adding that many Everest climbers have developed a "rather horrifying" attitude in which the zeal for reaching the summit has eclipsed even the most basic human values.[6]

We can only speculate as to why so many people denied help to Sharp. The bottom line is that a large number of people made the decision to put their personal desires or needs above Sharp's agonizing predicament. Missing from Sharp's final moments was the "love your neighbor as yourself"[7] standard.

But if we put ourselves in the place of the other climbers that day, we can see just how difficult it might have been to practice the "love your neighbor" standard. The benchmark Jesus established for love is not easy to live up to.

According to news reports, at least one or two people did try to help Sharp. How long Sharp had been in trouble before they arrived is not known. When they found him, he was close to death. Doctors say that when either cerebral or pulmonary edema advances beyond a certain point, supplementary oxygen and medications often don't help.[8] Nevertheless, the climber or climbers who stopped sent out a distress signal and tried to give him oxygen. But to carry Sharp down the mountain would have been impossible, they said.

Perhaps the other forty climbers didn't stop to help because they thought it would endanger their own lives. To be fair, the temperature earlier that morning had reached a deadly minus 100 degrees Fahrenheit. Also, when a person is at such high altitudes, he only has a limited amount of time in which he can stay in the "death zone" (above 26,000 feet) before the lack of oxygen becomes dangerous.[9] Sometimes even a small delay on Everest can mean the end, because storms move in and trap climbers so quickly. Seeing such peril, perhaps they decided it was too risky to help Sharp.[10]

Or, maybe Hillary's perspective is correct, and the climbers didn't help Sharp just because they wanted to ensure that they could make the summit. It costs tens of thousands of dollars to organize an Everest expedition, plus months of preparation and planning. After having ascended so far, to forgo the glory of reaching the top of the world's highest mountain in order to help Sharp may have seemed like a price too high to pay.

It's also possible that the climbers believed that Sharp was responsible for his own death. Sharp understood the risks he was taking when he decided to climb Everest. He must have known that 190 of the 1,500 or so climbers who have attempted to summit Everest have died since Hillary first succeeded in 1953. That is the risk one has to assume, something that all Everest climbers understand. And if that's understood, should the others on the mountain be required to risk their own lives or undermine their own objectives in order to rescue a sick person? From this point of view, Sharp's death is lamentable, but he alone was responsible.

All these excuses are rational and persuasive. We can understand how they would quickly lead the climbers to sidestep the command of Jesus to love one another. But regardless of how good the excuses were, David Sharp died. On the surface, we like what Jesus taught. We all agree that love is good. Who can argue with that? But if we encounter a situation in which love requires us to do something sacrificial, well, then we squirm.

Most of us will never face something like the drama of Sharp's death on Everest, but we will face the same tensions about love that the climbers faced. We all have our own mountains to climb, and we all hope to experience the glory of reaching the summit of our plans and dreams. We push and shove our way through today's frantic race to achieve personal success and a more comfortable life. In this competitive world, it is easy to be so consumed with reaching the peak of our objectives that we become impervious to the needs of others. Recognizing our fragile condition in a hostile financial and professional environment, we fear that helping others could lead to our demise. In a culture that thrives on radical individualism, such a lifestyle is even affirmed.

Each of us has an unavoidable, crucial choice: Are we going to live for others or for ourselves? The Scriptures teach that this choice will not only determine whether our lives are meaningful or empty but whether or not the fabric of our society will hold together.

TWO TOUGH FACTS ABOUT LOVE

The Scriptures teach us two facts about love. First, according to Paul in 1 Corinthians 13, no matter how talented and successful we might be, without love we and everything we do will amount to *nothing*. Even if I could move mountains, he says, if I "have not love, I am nothing."[11] For us in a twenty-first century culture of meritocracy, his words mean that technological advancement, dramatic growth of knowledge and information, and spectacular economic wealth mean nothing if we fail to love one another.

Paul is not saying that professional and technological advancement has no value. He is saying that if love doesn't infuse, motivate, and direct those things, our lives become empty shells. Without love, we end up like Sharp, having reached the summit of our achievements and yet found ourselves alone, freezing, without air to breathe, and dying. What difference do our achievements make if there is no love?

Stephen Kanitz, a columnist for the Brazilian news magazine *Veja*, tells about a lunch he had with a wealthy, workaholic businessman, during which he noticed a small tear forming in the man's eye. Then, during dessert, the man began to cry copiously. He explained to Kanitz that his daughter was about to get married and that only now had he realized that he didn't know her as a person. "I dedicated all my time to my business and I forgot to dedicate myself to my family," the man said through his tears.[12]

For most people, work is an expression of love, a means of providing for our families. But Kanitz calls into question the workaholic's all-consuming pursuit of material wealth that deprives families of the personal, human attention they so desperately need. He criticizes businesses that demand excessive hours from employees. The businessman who cried over his dessert realized that he had not found the right balance. As a result, he was experiencing the nothingness that grips our hearts when we fail to make love the central motivation of our lives.

The second fact the Scriptures teach about love is that it will always demand some degree of self-sacrifice. True love requires us to move beyond our self-interests and to give of ourselves in order to invest in others.

"To put the family in first place has a cost that not everyone is willing to pay," said Kanitz, in the same column. "It implies less money, less fame, less social projection. Many of your friends will become rich, more famous than you and will one day look down on you with disdain. In these hours it's consoling to remember that old saying that defines well why putting the family first is worth the cost: 'No success in life is worth a failure in the home.'"[13]

When we put both facts about love side by side, we see that to embrace life's meaning will mean a life of sacrifice. Therefore, love generates an inevitable tension in our hearts. First we learn that the meaning and purpose of life exists wholly within the context of love. Although we long for love and recognize its importance, we also shun it because it requires selfless living. The human heart has a love-hate relationship with love.

There is a paradoxical beauty to sacrificial love. The Bible never calls us to *pursue* suffering and sacrifice as an end in itself. What we find in the Scriptures are people who were committed first of all to truth and love. And sometimes this commitment led to suffering. The call to live for the sake of others, therefore, is not a call to self-neglect or self-deprecation. God has made each of us with our own personality, gifts, and talents. The call to love is a call to invest our lives and all that God has provided for the sake of others. It is a call to abandon a self-centered, egotistical, narcissistic life, not the inner person he created. *Rather than abolishing the person, God is interested in giving us each an abundant and full life.*[14]

But how can having an abundant, joyful life be reconciled with God's call to be "living sacrifices?" Here is the paradox of selfless love: By giving away our lives in service to others, we actually gain the fullness of life. The less we pursue self-interest and the more we love others, the more we embrace the riches of the meaningful life God designed for humankind. The more we believe and practice this, the more we experience a resulting pleasure and satisfaction.

Jesus said, "If anyone wishes to come after Me, he must deny himself, and take up his cross daily and follow Me."[15] To deny ourselves and take up our cross means to put aside our selfish pursuits so that we might serve others in love. While that might *seem* like a recipe for self-demise, we actually enter a fuller existence than we would ever find in a self-centered life.

Jesus proclaimed the paradox of love this way: "For whoever wishes to save his life will lose it, but whoever loses his life for My sake, he is the one who will save it. For what is a man profited if he gains the whole world, and loses or forfeits himself?"[16] The victorious paradox is that love enables people to blossom. Relationships will flourish, and our own lives will be filled with meaning.

LOVE: PASSION IN ACTION

Someone slipped an adoring, poetic, and sometimes erotic set of love letters between the despairing lament of Ecclesiastes and the prophetic words of Isaiah. It's called the Song of Solomon. About his wife, Solomon wrote,

> How much better is your love than wine,
>> And the fragrance of your oils
>> Than all kinds of spices!
> Your lips, my bride, drip honey;
>> Honey and milk are under your tongue.

. . . .

> Nard and saffron, calamus and cinnamon,
>> With all the trees of frankincense,
>> Myrrh and aloes, along with all the finest spices.
> You are a garden spring,
>> A well of fresh water,
>> And streams flowing from Lebanon.[17]

She is just as passionate about him:

> Awake, O north wind,
>> And come, wind of the south;
>> Make my garden breathe out fragrance,
>> Let its spices be wafted abroad.
>> May my beloved come into his garden
>> And eat its choice fruits![18]

Without this vibrant, emotional passion, marriage would be about as exciting as a day in traffic court. God made passion and romance. It's his invention, and we should nourish it. Even beyond marriage, God wants our relationships to be emotionally fulfilling, spontaneous, fun, adventurous, and dynamic.

Love is the greatest source of joy, pleasure, and sometimes pain. Whereas integrity can be dispassionate and objective and still remain true to itself, this is not the case with love. It could be argued that love in its truest form involves the mind, the will, and the emotions. It should involve the whole person. If love is only emotional, which is so often the case today, it will lack the staying power and permanence that people need. But if there is no emotional involvement, the relationship will be dry and lifeless. The many manifestations of love reveal how it can encompass every facet of human nature.

LOVE IS PHYSICAL

Love touches through handshakes, hugs, kisses, and sex. While there are cultural and personal differences, the lack of touch often suggests the lack of love. The popular press has reported how infants fail to thrive when they are not lovingly held and caressed. In adulthood, the need for friendly, loving touch is just as important. I (David) have clients who grieve deeply because for years no one has shown them physical affection. Their body aches from its absence. The thought of it produces an unimaginable longing.

Yet touch is so powerful that it must be used as an expression of the true relationship, not as a form of manipulation, aggression, or selfish desire. The way we touch one another needs to match the nature of the relationship. What's acceptable will vary between cultures and individuals, but the principle is universal. A hug between coworkers that lasts a second or two longer than "normal" can be confusing, threatening, or offensive. A stiff, brief hug with a spouse signifies distance and estrangement. Sex without committed love and unity leaves people feeling empty or used.

Love is expressed by physical proximity. You can tell much about a relationship by how closely people sit, walk, or stand together. There is a space between people that is invisible, but the people involved know what is happening between them.

The term for this is *proxemics*, coined by researcher Edward T. Hall in his 1966 book, *The Hidden Dimension*.[19] According to Hall, the closest space around a person is reserved for the closest friends and intimates. Greater love generates an increased desire for nearness.

My wife Linda and I (David) often tell our kids (the ones in late adolescence) how eager we are to have them at home. They often don't see the point of being at home when we aren't *doing* anything, but for us, the point is to be near them, in the same room. When you are apart from someone you love, there is no change in the love, but life feels empty because his or her body is not near. A person who believes he will one day be united with loved ones lost to death will still feel tremendous sorrow as a result of the physical separation.

LOVE PRODUCES EMOTIONAL JOY

I (David) once saw a tattoo on a woman's arm that said "Love Stinks." What a mistaken idea. Love doesn't stink. *Rejection* stinks. Love is possibly the deepest pleasure known to mankind. It captivates us and fills us with joy. We spend our lives seeking it. To be lost in the experience of love—that is a taste of heaven.

Perhaps God designed the pleasure and emotion of love to reward its presence. It is one of the strongest evidences that God exists. The pleasure of love compels us toward the eternal. Only the darkest cynics reduce love to biology. It is more than nature, more than matter, more than chemistry. Love makes us feel like we have become more than we are.

LOVE REFLECTS OUR HIERARCHY OF VALUES

Every parent knows the feeling of being in a store and losing a child. Parents will leave everything behind as they desperately search for the child. At that moment, everything else becomes worthless. Love reveals our deepest values. This explains why we feel threatened if someone else grows in favor with our friend. It is why we are jealous for our spouse. It is why marriages cannot be compromised without devastating consequences to the heart. It is the meaning of the first commandment, "You shall have no other gods before me."[20]

LOVE PURSUES THE BELOVED

Through my counseling practice, I (David) have heard thousands of life stories. There are some stories that evoke deep sadness. Usually they are told by people who were never pursued by others. Some people have childhood memories of when they deliberately hid from parents and waited for hours, but no one came to look for them. They experienced prolonged loneliness and grief. Conversely, one of the greatest joys is to be sought out, to be the one picked, hired, courted, and desired. For a friend, child, and spouse to realize that you can't wait to see them again is a profound expression of love. When a wife invites her husband out for a surprise lunch, she pursues him. When a father takes time off work to spend a day skiing with his son, the child can feel almost like nobility. When a friend invites you out for coffee just to hear how you are really doing, you feel loved.

LOVE IS PATIENT AND IT PERSEVERES

Teenage "first loves" are often remarkable experiences. We sometimes call it puppy love or infatuation. But that type of love is missing something essential—perseverance. Although the expression of love may be sincere, love is by nature a promise. This promise must be made carefully and kept steadfastly.

Love is devoted to the beloved, not just in marriage and family but also in friendship. It leads us to see the beloved and commit to them for the length of the journey. It stands with them through their grief and pain as well as their joy. This is the comfort of the central New Testament message. God loves you, and his love is permanent. Love's permanence is about the character of the lover not the beloved.

I (David) witnessed a beautiful example of unyielding love when my father-in-law died in 2004. At the moment he died, the whole family was in the hospital room. We comforted one another for a while by his bed, and then it became clear that it was time to leave the room. Everyone left except for my mother-in-law, Dorothy. She lingered behind the rest of us, and I heard her say to her husband, "You were the love of my life." These were the words of a woman whose love for her husband never ceased.

LOVE IS PROTECTIVE

Love acts on behalf of the beloved. It means buckling your child's safety seat. It refuses to let friends or family get drunk and drive. It means staying healthy for your spouse and children. It leads to teaching our children about the dangers of life and how to be wise in this world. It is looking out for the long-term interests of the people in our lives.

Love also protects the relationship itself as something sacred. It leads us to repair the relationship when damage has occurred. Love prompts us to apologize and to seek solutions to the sources of conflict rather than to withdraw. Love negotiates and adjusts expectations, and it drops the need to have things our own way. It releases self-interested control. Love shuts up and listens. It doesn't nag or get petty. It doesn't dominate or become passive. It is intolerant of estrangement.

LOVE VALUES AND ENJOYS PERSONALITY DIFFERENCES

John Gottman, a psychologist and author who has researched marital problems for more than twenty years, describes how conflict between married couples often emerges because of "dissimilar emotional lessons men and women learn in childhood." A man usually wants to "contain uncomfortable emotions—and avoid his wife's," whereas a woman wants to "express and manage a complete range of feelings."

Gottman went on to say, "When a woman looks for the same intimacy with her husband that she has experienced with female friends, she may be sorely disappointed. Likewise, a man who hopes to duplicate his 'buddy' relationships with his wife may feel overwhelmed by her need to talk about feelings or for emotional intimacy."[21]

These differences between men and women are actually good. Both traits are needed in a family. But in order to build marital intimacy in the context of these differences, both husband and wife must move toward the other. Each person must learn to recognize and appreciate the diverse qualities that he or she brings to the marriage, and then each must take action to relate to the other according to each person's unique personality. Love transforms our differences into a source of strength—and *delight* — rather than a source of conflict.

LOVE IS A VERB

What you find in all these manifestations of love is one common denominator: Love serves. Not long before his death, Jesus had a meal with his friends. He knew that he would be arrested and taken to the cross soon. He wanted to show them how much he loved them, and he wanted to teach them how to care for one another. So he dressed with a towel around his waist, which in those days was the attire of a servant or slave, and he washed their feet. In this act, Jesus showed us that the essence of love is serving. It is active. But it is full of passion and sincerity, not without emotion. It puts the self second and others first and then moves to tangibly remedy the needs of others.

I (Jim) have been married to my wife, Marge, for fifty-three years (at this writing). We are still intimate friends and immensely enjoy life together. But that did not just happen. During our first ten years together, I was oblivious to what it meant to really love my wife. Sure, we "loved" each other. We had a strong commitment to the marriage. That was like money in the bank, and I knew I could draw on it. We got along and had fun together, so I didn't think much about how little I was *investing* in my wife's well-being.

Then we moved. We didn't just change cities and jobs, we changed countries and languages. There is nothing like a cross-cultural change of that magnitude to bring the things that are deep inside a person to the surface, for better or for worse.

We settled in the provincial city of Curitiba, Brazil, and began to set up our household. As the months passed, I observed Marge withdraw and wither. Finally it dawned on me. She had been cut off from everything and everyone that had nourished her. Her friends were gone. She was caring for two small children, which further decreased her contact with the rest of the world. She was receiving little or no relational or spiritual nourishment from anyone.

I also became aware of several bad relational habits that today I am ashamed to remember. I would belittle her with cutting remarks disguised as humor. And I was so goal-oriented that I would roll over whatever was in the way, even my own wife.

When she couldn't take it anymore, she blew up. We were in our car on a mountain road in southern Brazil. (Forty years later, I could still find the spot on the road where it happened.) She let me know what I was doing to her and how she felt about it. And, for the first time in my life, I heard her. Sure, I had heard the same words from her before, but this time I *heard* her. But what was I to do?

I was standing in our living room alone one day when a phrase out of the New Testament popped into my mind, "Husbands, love your wives, just as Christ loved . . . and gave himself up . . . to present her . . . without stain or wrinkle or any other blemish."[22] It was an epiphany! Marge was *my* responsibility, and I needed to act accordingly.

Jesus, our model, gave up his life for our benefit. He took *action*, putting aside all selfish concerns. And that was what I needed to do for Marge. I began to consciously work at being alert to her needs and to be there to meet them. I began to invest in her, rather than just taking our marital commitment for granted.

I'm still at it. I have a daily choice to make in our marriage. I ask myself, are you going to love Marge today? I know that to say "yes" will cost me time and energy. It will mean staying alert to what's happening in her life and taking initiatives to make her day better. It often comes down to simple acts of service in the course of the day.

There can be no love without action. We often think that as long as we mind our own business and don't hurt anyone, we can do whatever we want. But the "love your neighbor as yourself" principle leads us to be proactive in our relationships. If we take those words seriously, there is no way we can see a person in need and then just feel pity. Love is more than a compassionate feeling. Loving your neighbor means being an active servant.

To be a servant, as Jesus modeled, requires humility. He dressed as a slave and kneeled down before his friends, even though he is the highest authority in the universe. In this way he showed that love is also inseparable from humility, just as it is inseparable from integrity. Humility is the topic of the next chapter.

QUESTIONS FOR DISCUSSION

1. The chapter begins with the statement that truth and love are an amalgam and that one depends on the other. How do you understand that? What happens when truth is used apart from love? What happens to love where truth is not present?

2. The apostle Paul, in 1 Corinthians 13, identifies love as the greatest of all virtues. He states that all achievements, no matter how noble, sacrificial, or spectacular they might be, are nothing if love is absent. That's a pretty radical statement. How would you interpret it?

3. What makes loving another so difficult?

4. Because love is a verb, it will be expressed through action. Does that also mean that love is a choice? Can I just *choose* to love a person?

5. Are there aspects of love that were not mentioned that seem essential to you? Can you describe them?

Chapter 7

HUMILITY

On that Wyoming night under the stars I (Glenn) described in an earlier chapter, the immensity of space declared my finitude. I realized that I was a pinpoint, a grain of sand, a needle in a haystack, a speck of dust, maybe even a sub-atomic particle in comparison to the whole.

But while the heavens declared my smallness before an omnipotent God, I did not feel insignificant. The scene was too beautiful for me to feel that way. The starry array was alluring, drawing me beyond my pre-adolescent world of school, Batman, and tetherball championships. Beauty seemed to be God's way of saying, "I know you." I remember feeling immense joy.

The more I have learned about the universe, the more I'm amazed. Consider the star called Betelgeuse, a variable red giant that marks the left shoulder of the constellation Orion. Scientists say that if this star were placed at the center of our solar system, it would stretch to the orbit of Jupiter. That means it is approximately 600 million miles wide. The outer edge of the star's circumstellar envelope, which is a shell of gas around the star, extends over a trillion kilometers beyond the star itself. It takes about two months for the star's light to escape from its own shell.[1]

As you try to get your mind around those dimensions, remember that Betelgeuse is only one star among an estimated 10,000 billion billion stars in about 100 billion galaxies.[2]

This is pure speculation, but perhaps God made the universe to be so enormous and grand just so that he could hold human pride in check. Maybe he wanted us to look at the heavens and say, "Who do I think I am, anyway?" The whole shebang is conceivably God's way of reminding us that mankind's greatest feats and inventions are but a trifle. What is the world's tallest skyscraper next to Betelgeuse? Van Gogh's painting *Starry Night* is splendid, but how does it stack up next to the beauty of a supernova? Nuclear power generators are certainly a demonstration of humans' scientific prowess, but think of the sun, which fuses 660 million tons of hydrogen into helium and energy every second.[3] Some modern nations have achieved remarkable technological advancement, but what is all that compared to the perfect functional complexity of a human red blood cell?

Christians and atheists agree on at least one point: Humans are miniscule when compared to time and space. The atheists tend to use this fact as evidence against the existence of a personal God. But the Christian perspective says that there is more to our story than just our size. The miracle of life, the beauty of creation, and the fact that the universe is fine-tuned for life on Earth are evidence that humankind is valuable in the eyes of the Creator. We might be dust, but we are also loved, valued, and known dust. The logical response to God's majesty should be awestruck humility.

But when the Scriptures teach us about our need for humility, they never diminish the value of each person. To the contrary, our worth has been declared by God. The Christian faith is the only faith that establishes humanity's immeasurable value and simultaneously gives us no basis for pride. That's because God loves us not as a result of our performance, talents, wealth, or appearance but because of his grace.

The word *grace* signifies something that is received without cost or merit. In Spanish, people say *gracias* after receiving a gift. When something is free, people who speak Portuguese say it is *de graça*. Pure and simple, grace is the act of giving and receiving a gift that can't be earned. It's the opposite of receiving a salary, which is something you worked for and deserve. God's love is a gift, not a trophy. For this reason Paul writes that we "are justified [made right] *freely by his grace* through the redemption that came by Christ Jesus."[4] Merit is not part of the equation.

For this reason God's love is difficult to accept. A merit-based approach to life gives us a theoretical right to be prideful. Grace, by contrast, eliminates the basis for pride. Paul made this very clear. If Jesus has done all the work to make us right before God, and we have done nothing to earn it, "Where, then, is boasting?" he asked. To that question Paul answered, "It is excluded."[5]

As a result, we are both attracted to grace and uncomfortable with it. An internal battle emerges between the desires of the human ego and our desire for God's unconditional love. When grace invades our pride, something deep within us prefers a life of performance—as exhausting as that can be—because we want to be able to put a trophy in our display case.

Frederick Buechner said that God is to mankind a "beloved enemy." He is beloved because of his generosity. But he is also an enemy because he declares his rightful authority over our lives. To be filled with God's life, there must be, Buechner said, a "magnificent defeat of the human soul at the hands of God."[6] The defeat of pride is magnificent because it is then that we recognize our need for God and become receptive to the true life he offers. And when we truly accept the gift of God, we find inner rest. The hard labor of proving our worth comes to an end.

"It is just when we realize that it is impossible by any effort of our own to make ourselves children and thus to enter the kingdom of heaven that we become children . . . not because we try and not because we recognize the futility of our trying; but simply because he has chosen to love us," wrote Buechner.[7]

This childlike humility is the starting point for all healthy relationships, first with God and then with one another. If we fail to recognize our smallness before God and our desperate need for his grace, then pride, which by nature is self-centered and competitive, will dominate our actions and attitudes. The result will be relational brokenness.

THE PRIDE IN OUR VEINS

Like an undertow in the ocean, pride affects our relationships in ways that we often don't recognize until it has pulled us far from shore. It's an invisible force, but it's strong and dangerous.

Pride has been destroying relationships since Adam and Eve. The foolish desire to be like God, to be autonomous and independent, drew them into deadly waters. Following the humanistic spirit, they asserted a reign of self-sufficiency. God had already given them tremendous freedom. But all they had received from God wasn't enough. They wanted to be like God, and they were prideful enough to believe they *could* be like him.

In this we see that pride is a form of delusion. The lie on which they gambled their lives crumbled to the ground, and they ended up ashamed, divided, and lost. The relational intimacy they once had with God and with one another became a life filled with fear, judgment, and hiding. Rather than humbly assume responsibility for the consequences, they cast blame on God and on one another.

The invisible pull of pride affects us in many ways. We feel the consequences of it, but we rarely identify pride as the cause. It appears in our lives from a very early age, when we begin comparing ourselves to one another and looking for ways to gain the attention of our peers. We unwittingly adopt a belief that our talents, attire, appearance, and intelligence are the means to move up the social ladder and generate our self-worth. Thus, pride, which is fundamentally competitive, turns our focus inward to selfish objectives and away from the needs of others. The focus of life becomes self-promotion in relation to others. Pride makes us discontent with equality, envious of others, frustrated by inferiority, and driven toward supremacy.

One tactic of self-promotion commonly seen among school-age children is the attempt to devalue one's peers. Bullying is rampant. Sometimes it is physical. More often it involves verbal put-downs and social marginalization. But the motive of all bullying is to make oneself feel superior by physically or verbally demeaning others. It is a cheap form of self-promotion.

By the time most people reach high school, the social comparisons make them highly self-conscious. Some are able to hide their fears with athletic prowess and academic achievement. But most must search for other external props that can help them in the struggle to feel accepted and valued.

This same self-promotional ethos continues to motivate us in subtle ways as we move through college and into our professions. In the American perspective in recent decades, work has been increasingly tied to generating the value of a person's identity. Work is often believed to be the means to "make something of myself." The down side of this approach is that unemployment not only undermines financial security, it sabotages the person's sense of self-worth.

Where we most feel the painful outcome of pride is in our relationships with those closest to us. Stanley Fish, a literary theorist and professor, wrote a light-hearted but insightful column for the *New York Times* about what happens in domestic quarrels. Although he never cited pride as the underlying cause of these household battles, he showed that many of our conflicts are not caused by a substantive disagreement but rather by an arrogant attitude. One person interprets an innocuous comment or action as an offense. Then the conversation spirals toward anger and division.

"The provoker — or, rather, the person accused of being one — will immediately claim innocence: 'I was just asking a simple question. Why did you think I meant *that*? I would never mean *that*,'" Fish wrote, showing how the accused person manages to turn the tables on the accuser. Then he added, "The claim of innocence is itself not so innocent; it is at bottom an accusation of the other for having not only misunderstood an irreproachable intention, but for having impugned an irreproachable character."[8]

Pride is the underlying cause of this typical rift. The "claim of innocence" springs forth from an arrogant view of the self. It is rooted in the assumption of "an irreproachable character" — that there can be no wrong in me. Then, as a means of staying in a position of moral or intellectual superiority, each person criticizes the other. There are times when matters of importance cause conflict, but more often than not arguments erupt and continue to wreak havoc because of pride.

John Gottman's extensive research on marriages also shows how pride is the primary culprit of marital collapse. He identified what he calls the "four horsemen of the apocalypse," which are the principle four factors that lead to divorce.

The first is *criticism*, which "involves attacking someone's personality or character—rather than a specific behavior—usually with blame."[9]

The second horseman is *contempt*, which takes criticism to a more severe level, having "the intention to insult and psychologically abuse your partner." With contempt "you're lobbing insults right into the heart of your partner's sense of self." The person voices angry judgments that his or her partner is "stupid, disgusting, incompetent, and a fool."[10]

The third horseman is *defensiveness*, which is characterized by the denial of personal responsibility, making excuses, returned accusations, reversing the blame, and even whining. The problem with defensiveness, said Gottman, is that it obstructs communication. "Rather than understanding each other's perspective you spend your discussions defending yourselves."[11]

The final horseman, *stonewalling*, is the worst of all. "The stonewaller just removes himself by turning into a stone wall," Gottman said. "It conveys disapproval, icy distance, and smugness," and it can mark the end of communication and possibly the end of a relationship.[12]

Each horseman is an expression of pride.

The fact is that in most relational conflicts, everyone is a victim and no one is innocent. But in the heat of the battle, pride blinds us to our own failures and amplifies the injustices others have committed against us.

"Research teaches us that our reasons [for retaliation] and our pains [inflicted by others] are more palpable, more obvious and real, than are the reasons and pains of others," said Daniel Gilbert. "This leads to the escalation of mutual harm, to the illusion that others are solely responsible for it and to the belief that our actions are justifiable responses to theirs."[13]

Jesus said the same thing long ago, when he warned us against judging others for the speck of sawdust in their eye without seeing the plank in our own eye.[14] If pride is a principal source of relational division, then obviously humility is the starting place and foundation for unity.

In reality, the step toward humility is not a one-time event. Our experience with pride is that it is a constant battle. As adults we become more aware of our pride than when we were school kids hoping to find a place on the social ladder. But does that make us more humble? And even if we have humbled ourselves, we soon find that we're proud of our humility. It's like the old joke, in which a man says: "I used to be arrogant, but now I'm perfect."

C. S. Lewis wrote, "If anyone would like to acquire humility, I can, I think, tell him the first step. The first step is to realize that one is proud. And a biggish step, too. At least, nothing whatever can be done before it. If you think you are not conceited, it means you are very conceited indeed."[15]

Nevertheless, we are called to move in the right direction, even if imperfectly. Jesus is, once again, a perfect model for us to follow in our relationships.

JESUS AND HUMILITY

The humility of Jesus is an extraordinary paradox. He was the Lord of the Universe, the Creator of the cosmos, the author of life, God himself in a human body. He could have come to earth with unprecedented opulence and grandeur. Instead he spent his first days in a feeding trough for animals, born to poor parents who had to wrap him in rags. For the next two years he lived as a refugee hiding from a paranoid king who hoped to murder him. After that he grew up in a small, impoverished village, working with his father as a carpenter. The contrast between his true identity and the form he adopted for his life on earth is incomprehensible.

Thus, on the one hand, the people who had direct contact with Jesus saw a simple person living a simple life. There was nothing noble about his upbringing or education. He was not wealthy. But then, when his work on earth began in earnest, he made huge claims about his deity, power, and purpose.

Not surprisingly, he became the source of much discussion and debate. To some people, Jesus was indeed the Son of God, and these people followed him to the end. To others, he was demon-possessed or crazy. We don't find any examples in the New Testament of people saying that he was just a nice guy with good morals and happy teachings, as many people believe today.

In other words, if what Jesus said about himself were false, he would have been a man who had reached the apex of lunacy and delusion. But if what he said about himself were true, then he was the most humble man to ever walk the planet. For he was the Creator himself, stepping into time and space to submit under the weight of the brutal Roman government, to live under the roof of a poor man's home, and finally to face the death of a common criminal. No one could have made a larger leap of humility—from the heavens to the cross.

The humility of Jesus affected people in different ways. He attracted the humble and repelled the prideful. Songwriter Bruce Cockburn poetically captured this truth in these lyrics about the birth of Jesus:

There are others who know about this miracle birth
The humblest of people catch a glimpse of their worth
For it isn't to the palace that the Christ child comes
But to shepherds and street people,
Hookers and bums.[16]

Jesus said in the Beatitudes that those who are poor in spirit, those who mourn, those who are meek, those who hunger and thirst for righteousness, are actually blessed.[17] What a contrast to the standards of today's world! Why would he say that? Because this humble position before God, the recognition of our needy condition, is the first step toward healthy relationships.

The first four beatitudes describe an inner state of humility: To be poor in spirit gives way to mourning over the brokenness of our souls and the condition of the world; mourning gives way to meekness, which produces a spiritual hunger and thirst for what is good and right. The next three beatitudes describe an outward way of life that stems from inner humility.[18] Those who are humble will be merciful with others. They will be pure in heart, which means to be fully focused on God. God's heart is set on reconciling humanity to himself, and so the pure in heart are peacemakers, people whose goal in life is to bring about relational unity from what has been broken by sin.

Interestingly, the last beatitude says that as a result of this right way of living, it's possible that we will be persecuted.[19] That's because such a life runs counter to the prideful ethos of the world.

THE RELATIONAL POWER OF HUMILITY

What image comes to mind when you think of a humble person? If you are like most people, humility is often equated with weakness and resignation. So the idea of being humble seems like a recipe for failure in a competitive world. To succeed, we think it is necessary to live like a running back, ready to barrel over anyone who gets in the way.

But consider Jesus. He was humble, but he wasn't weak. If you consider the responsibility that he assumed, one can't help but be amazed at his courage. By his own volition, he handed himself to the authorities and allowed himself to be hung on the cross. He was the good shepherd who, when the wolves entered the sheep pen to attack, sacrificed his life to protect them. The real cowards were the hired hands who bolted when their own lives were at stake. Jesus lived for what was right and holy, even when it meant rejection and abuse. He directed his life away from self-interest, a true measure of strength. His focus was to fulfill God's purposes of love, to provide personal care for each individual he encountered, and to establish a movement that would transform world history.

But he accomplished all this through humility. He always *submitted* to the will of his Father. He *served* others instead of seeking his own glory. In the account of his temptation, he refused to succumb to the allure of pride and maintained his allegiance to his Father. Even his victory over all the evil imposed upon him was accomplished in a moment of ultimate humility—his death by a brutal means reserved for criminals. Jesus was purposeful, directed, motivated, passionate, and courageous. In all these examples, Jesus reveals that true humility is powerful not weak and aimless.

Jesus' way of life is still relevant to contemporary business practices. Author Jim Collins, in his book about the most successful businesses, identified humility as a common characteristic of the best high-level leaders. Humility, he says, is a trait that makes business leaders able to build and run great companies: "[The greatest] leaders channel their ego needs away from themselves and into the larger goal of building a great company. . . . Their ambition is first and foremost for the institution, not themselves."[20]

Collins and his research team discovered that the people who had worked with or written about these high-level leaders described them with words such as *humble, modest, shy, gracious, mild-mannered,* and *self-effacing.* Yet they are determined and passionate. They are humble but also brave. And they are highly concerned about the long-term future of the company rather than their own wealth and fame.

"[The best] leaders want to see the company even more successful in the next generation, and they are comfortable with the idea that most people won't even know that the roots of that success traces back to their efforts," said Collins.[21]

The relational power of humility comes from its link to integrity and love. Humility is, in fact, the door that opens before the character traits of integrity and love can be formed in a person.

As humility clears the way for a life of integrity and love, relational stability grows. When families, friendships, and professional partnerships function on the basis of humility, most conflicts are eliminated before they ever start. Pride, however, usually leads to conflict.

The prideful person will jump to a conclusion, make a decision, and then act without ever considering how it might affect the others involved. As a result, he leaves a trail of wounded people in his wake. But the humble person recognizes that his own understanding could be misguided, leading him to seek counsel from others, including God, before making decisions. The humble person doesn't demand immediate results or absolute perfection from others. In the best marriages, husband and wife work toward mutual agreements. Marriage ceases to be a struggle for power and control and becomes a team effort to survive the storms of life together.

In the midst of differing opinions, the humble person will recognize his or her own intellectual limits and therefore appreciate the perspectives of others. Humility transforms communication, removing the prideful demand to be right all the time and encouraging people to listen carefully to one another. It deepens mutual understanding, whereas pride leads to judgment and criticism.

Humility removes competition and envy. The humble person prefers to promote others and to encourage them rather than to compete against them. By removing the need to be better than others, humility also brings inner peace and contentment to the heart of the humble person.

Not all conflicts, of course, can be prevented. We may experience the pain of separations and bitter disputes. However, when such division has occurred, humility is the first step toward appeasement. It leads us to confession and apology.

When my wife and I quarrel, I (David) will notice an internal opposition to the idea that I should apologize. But Linda has never responded negatively to an apology, which shows me the absurdity of my reluctance to apologize. My resistance to humility makes no sense.

Perhaps the deepest expression of humility's power to heal relationships is confession. Confession is one of the hardest things for us to accomplish. Our natural tendency is to rationalize our actions, to lie, and to cast blame on others. But when confession happens, intimacy is given a new chance to grow. Some of the most beautiful times between people happen in moments of confession and repentance.

In all these ways, we find that humility is a powerful force for relational health. It is courageous, purposeful, focused on serving others, and uninterested in personal glory. As humility opens the door to integrity and love, this attitude works to eliminate the causes of most relational conflict before the cracks between us can expand into chasms. And even when there is a major fracture, humility is a powerful healing and restorative force.

SPIRITUAL BLINDNESS AND PRIDE

Pride is spiritual blindness. To be arrogant is to live in the delusion of self-reliance, to believe that we don't need God. An elevated view of the self leads us to falsely imagine that we don't need others, either.

We see ourselves as always being right about everything. Therefore, we must have the last word in an argument. We approach conversations with a demeanor of superiority. We don't see any need to listen to others, because we believe that we already know it all.

What's worse about pride is that we usually don't even recognize that we're blind. For this reason Jesus did everything he could to help people recognize the vanity that kept them from seeing their need for God. The self-righteous religious leaders of the day once caught a woman in the act of adultery. This group of men brought the woman to Jesus and, trying to trap him, asked what should be done with her. The real problem was that pride had blinded them to their own flawed condition. So Jesus silently stooped to the ground, wrote something in the dirt, and said, "If any one of you is without sin, let him be the first to throw a stone at her." They all left the scene, humbled.[22]

This story is full of meaning for our relationships. Pride led the men to judge and condemn the woman, and it leads us to do the same thing in our relationships. If we see ourselves as being morally superior to others, we will easily criticize and reject those around us. But if we look at our true condition before God, we will realize that we don't have any basis to think of ourselves as better than others. At the same time, the humble person can still take a stand against what is morally wrong, just as Jesus did not approve of adultery and told the woman to turn away from such destructive behavior.

HUMILITY AND FEAR

In these competitive times, many people have a legitimate fear that others might take advantage of them or judge them. A prideful attitude often seems safer than humility. Pride is a way of minimizing our concern of being rejected or despised. In fact, pride is a response to our physical and spiritual vulnerability.

"In conditions of utmost physical security, we still must grow old and sometime die," wrote Glenn Tinder. "We do not know what this will mean to us. Nor, looking back, do we know how or why we have come to be. Hence we feel not only physically, but also metaphysically unsafe. We fear, beyond ineffectiveness, guilt and condemnation, and beyond loss of life, loss of soul."[23]

It is possible to respond to this fear of vulnerability with humility, increasing our dependency on God. But more often we respond with pride, which leads us to build up walls of defense, to pursue self-interest at the expense of those closest to us, to hide our fears with strong reactions. Pride becomes a multifaceted means by which we try to gain control over our lives and attempt to moderate our fragile condition. In relationships, this causes us to lie, to be self-seeking, to manipulate others for personal gain, to blame others in order to maintain a semblance of moral superiority, and even to deny the existence of a personal God to whom we must respond.

The irony is that pride actually creates the situations that we most dread. For example, the longing for self-rule and autonomy—a form of control aimed at self-protection—ends up separating us from God and others. This leaves our lives devoid of love and intimacy, which is one of our greatest fears. Pride, therefore, holds us in a vicious circle. Sooner or later, we begin to experience the painful consequences of our vain decisions provoked by fear. As David wrote, "He [man] has dug a pit and hollowed it out, and has fallen into the hole which he made."[24]

One of the best examples in the Bible of this pride-to-ruin pattern is Jesus' parable of the prodigal son in Luke 15. The son seeks his autonomy and, after a period of enjoyment, finds himself impoverished, lonely, empty, and feeding pigs that eat better than he does. His pursuit of freedom has led him to a barren life dominated by the consequences of his prideful decisions.

The beauty of the story is that humility frees him from the consequences of his selfishness. Remembering the joy and love he had at home with his father, he returns as a desperate, broken man dressed in rags. He recognizes the futility of his pride and turns toward home. This turnabout is the essence of humility. It is at once a magnificent defeat and a beautiful victory. It is the first step toward restored relationships.

But his relationship with his father does not depend only on the humility of the son. The son must face a frightening risk. Will the father accept such a wayward, miserable son who once rejected his father and squandered his hard-earned wealth?

The outcome depends on the father's willingness to forgive his son. Forgiveness is the subject of the next chapter.

QUESTIONS FOR DISCUSSION

1. What is humility? How is it expressed? How does humility interact with integrity and love?
2. Can you be humble and confident at the same time?
3. Why is humility essential to healthy relationships?
4. What does humility accomplish in a conflict resolution that nothing else can?
5. In contrast, what are the effects of pride on a conflict?

Chapter 8

FORGIVENESS

In the *sertão*, a large desert in northeastern Brazil, about thirty million people struggle to survive under the pounding sun. The faces of older people resemble the land that is cracked by drought and heat. Hundreds of small municipalities serve as commercial centers for poor rural workers, many of whom live in houses made with sticks and mud. Some families survive by sending the man of the house to the large cities in wealthier southern Brazil, where they find construction jobs in the urban sprawl. If possible, these workers send money back to their families in the desert. Meanwhile, the women left behind, who are called "widows of the drought," take care of the small farms, the animals, the children, and the elderly.

Beyond the economic struggles, the *nordestinos* have had to endure violent, long-running family battles that have left hundreds dead. In the town of Exu, a dispute between two politically powerful families set off a chain of retaliatory killings that lasted more than thirty years and caused the deaths of more than forty people. More recently, in 1989, a drug debt led to the murder of one young man in the town of Belem do São Francisco. Relatives of the victim decided to take revenge. The killing spree between the two families lasted fourteen years and left about 170 people dead. In the small town of Floresta do Navio, a battle between two families has been going on since the early 1900s.[1]

The causes of the violence are usually innocuous issues such as a local election, a small financial debt, a stolen goat. But once the first person is killed, the torturous wheel of revenge starts to roll. In most cases, the violence ends in one of three ways: when one side has been completely exterminated, when both parties eventually become weary of killing each other, or when a third party steps in with a peace treaty.

A strong sense of personal and family honor is the underlying motive of these battles. People here believe they must do everything necessary to maintain the honor of the family name, even if killing someone in revenge is required.[2] In the sertão, researchers say, revenge is about more than imposing justice; it is the way a family sustains its dignity. To forgive someone would, in their minds, dishonor one's family.

Forgiveness, however, is desperately needed. Generations have become caught in a cycle of anger and reprisal. Children grow up without their fathers and brothers. Women are left without husbands. Innocent young people go to early graves. Survivors often have bullet scars on their bodies. People live with daily fear that they could be the next target. Just having the wrong last name can be a ticket to the cemetery.

Unfortunately, the sertão is just one place in our broken world where forgiveness is needed. The need is universal. Nearly 595,000 people were murdered in the United States between 1976 and 2005.[3] That's an average of almost 20,000 people every year. And every person who died has left behind family and friends who quietly bear the emotional pain caused by such terrible offenses. How are people to cope? What do they do with the pain?

Most people never have to deal with the agonizing anger and hatred that can overwhelm a murder victim's family and friends. But almost everyone struggles, sometimes daily, with other offenses that cause deep wounds in our souls. A trusted friend takes the job you wanted by telling lies about your private life. Marital infidelity leaves a spouse feeling demeaned and rejected. A friend stops calling without explanation. A child is abused by a parent. Others suffer daily in manipulative and controlling marriages, often compounded by verbal ridicule. And the closer we are to someone, the more painful the insults can be.

Our friend John is a natural servant who loves to meet people's needs. So when his friend was facing bankruptcy, John set out to help him. He mentored his friend in personal money management and loaned him enough money to spare him from financial ruin.

John's generous nature led him to help other friends too. A few months later, one of them landed in financial trouble due to a business slump. Again, John provided the funds to help his friend. Then John, who was a builder, built a new home for a young couple in financial need.

Not long after these events, I (Jim) visited John and found him deeply saddened. I learned that he had suffered huge disappointments with all three of the friends he had so generously assisted. All of them had offended John in one way or another, even though he had done so much to help them. He found himself estranged from each of them. Naturally, he was confused, angry, and hurt. Dismay dominated his emotions and thoughts, leaving John in a serious spiritual crisis that lasted for a number of years.

Forgiveness was at the heart of John's struggle. A superficial understanding of forgiveness was not sufficient to ease his pain. Like John, we also need a solid understanding of the issue. Otherwise we will go through life chained to our pain and even perpetuating revenge.

THE NOT-SO-COMFORTING COUNSEL OF JESUS

Jesus is someone who understands what it means to live with injustice, offense, cruelty, ridicule, and all the other things that hurt our souls. He walked onto the stage of human history when life was brutal and unfair, especially for Jews trying to survive under the iron-fisted Roman government. Jesus could have chosen a nicer time and place to appear on the scene. But instead he put himself under a ruthless regime and ultimately submitted to the worst forms of oppression and injustice.

While Jesus deeply cares about our suffering, he never encourages us to wallow in self-pity and bitterness. Instead of giving us license to seek revenge on our enemies, we find him repeatedly talking about *our responsibility to forgive those who offend us*. He called us to forgive everyone—those who have insulted us, stolen our belongings, and even killed our relatives.

In order to define forgiveness for his friends, he told one of his trademark stories. A king had a servant, Jesus said, who had borrowed a huge sum of money from the king. In fact, the servant owed the king 10,000 talents of silver, or the equivalent of 930,000 pounds. At today's writing, that's worth more than $260 million. The king, wanting to recoup some of his losses, considered selling the man, his wife, children, and all their possessions. But the servant begged the king for patience. The king took pity on him, *canceled the debt, and let him go*.[4]

In this story, Jesus demonstrated what God has done for each of us. He has cancelled our debt. And he shows us that forgiveness is a deliberate choice to release another person from a debt.

Think carefully about what Jesus is saying: God calls the person who has suffered terrible loss—the person who has been defrauded in a business deal, the wife whose husband committed adultery, the family of a murder victim—to cancel the perpetrator's debt and release them. According to Jesus, forgiveness means that we set the offender free from the demand to repay us for what we've lost. And that means that we assume the weight of the debt.

If we're honest, forgiveness seems terribly unfair. It seems to contradict justice. Forgiveness is also exactly the last thing a person who has been deeply hurt by someone wants to do. Just when a person is reeling from the pain of loss and insult, Jesus comes along and talks about that person's responsibility to let the perpetrator go free. At every turn, forgiveness is counterintuitive.

One of our good friends recently went through a divorce after a long struggle with an unfaithful and demeaning husband. Beyond having to endure the tremendous pain of rejection, she was forced to raise her children without much help from the ex-husband. Her financial losses were sizeable, so she had to work longer hours and thus had less time with her kids. Under the pressures of finances and the needs of her children, the stress in her life increased exponentially.

In her understandable anger and frustration, she longed to see justice imposed on her ex-husband. She wanted retribution. One evening she asked us, "How is it that he can hurt me so much and then God asks me to let him off the hook? It's not fair!"

My wife and I (David) experienced a tragedy evoking this struggle a number of years ago when a seventeen-year-old boy murdered one of our best friends. She and her husband were in the process of moving to a different city. Her husband had just left town to report at a new job while she stayed behind to sell their home. One morning on the way to work, she was assaulted. When she fought back, the attacker struck her in the head and killed her. The police found him, he was tried as an adult, and they sent him to prison.

For a long time after her death, I carried the shock and rage around in my head nearly every day. During this period, a close friend and I were meeting to help each other grow and to share our struggles. Some time after the murder, we ended up talking about forgiveness. We made a list of people and began to pray and forgive. I finished praying through my list, but my friend noticed that something was missing. He asked, "What about the guy who killed your friend?" I sat upright and vehemently said, "I will not forgive him!"

My friend asked me what was keeping me from forgiving the man. I was repelled by the idea of forgiving someone who had done something so heinous and startled by the way the need for forgiveness upended my sense of justice.

Author and theologian Miroslav Volf is another man who understands the apparent unfairness of forgiveness. Volf is a Croatian university professor who taught in former Yugoslavia during the early 1990s. At that time, Serbian fighters, called *cetnik*, had been "herding people into concentration camps, raping women, burning down churches, and destroying cities." Volf's book *Exclusion and Embrace* is the result of his personal struggle to understand forgiveness in regard to the people who desolated his own nation and compatriots. In it he wrote,

> How does one remain loyal both to the demand of the oppressed for justice and to the gift of forgiveness that the Crucified offered to the perpetrators? I felt caught between two betrayals—the betrayal of the suffering, exploited, and excluded, and the betrayal of the very core of my faith. In a sense even more disturbingly,

I felt that my very faith was at odds with itself, divided between ... the demand to bring about justice for the victims and the call to embrace the perpetrator.[5]

Jesus knew that forgiveness was a difficult task. He never offered a pat answer for the tensions we feel between justice and forgiveness. But he didn't just talk about forgiveness; he modeled it. So when he asks us to follow him in forgiving others, he does so fully understanding the tension between forgiveness and fairness.

As Jesus was taking his last breaths, he cried out for the Father to forgive those who had pounded the nails into his hands and feet, to forgive those who had beaten him to a bloody pulp, to forgive those who had insulted him and pressed the crown of thorns on his head, and to forgive those involved in his unfair trial. As we know, he also assumed the entire load of sin for all mankind past, present, and future. He, like the king in the story, paid our entire debt. Was what happened to Jesus fair? Certainly not!

In the remainder of the story about the king and the servant, Jesus takes our question about the fairness of forgiveness to a deeper level. The story continues this way: After the king forgave the servant's debt, the servant encountered a colleague who owed him a hundred denarii, the equivalent of a laborer's wages for a hundred days of work. This too was no small debt, but it was far less than what the servant had owed the king. Unmoved by what the king had just done for him, the servant grabbed his fellow man by the throat and demanded full payment. The man begged the king's servant for patience, but he refused. Instead, the servant had the man thrown into prison.

News of this reached the king. He called for the servant and said to him, "You wicked servant. . . . I canceled all that debt of yours because you begged me to. Shouldn't you have had mercy on your fellow servant just as I had on you?"[6]

Then Jesus added an enigmatic ending to his story. He said, "In anger his master turned him over to the jailers to be tortured, until he should pay back all he owed. 'This is how my heavenly Father will treat each of you unless you forgive your brother from your heart.'"[7]

What an unforgiving ending to a story on forgiveness! But think about it. Jesus told this story to explain the nature of forgiveness. He said that if we truly understand and receive God's forgiveness it will make a dramatic difference in the way we treat others. When we, in humility, fully grasp the impossible debt God has forgiven on our behalf, a debt we could never begin to pay, it is incomprehensible for us not to forgive the offenses that others have committed against us. Jesus is saying that if we are unforgiving toward others, it reveals that we never understood God's forgiveness toward us. We never really grasped the depth of our own need to be forgiven. And without that we remain under the burden of our debt and all the judgment that comes with it.

We must live with whichever system we choose.

THE PROCESS OF FORGIVENESS

The act of forgiveness is rarely an immediate event. Arriving at a place of true forgiveness after we have been offended often takes time. Forgiveness is a process that involves the emotions, the mind, and the will. Each element of our being must move toward the decision to forgive.

The first reaction to an offense or injury is usually pain, anger, and outrage. We are offended by injustice. In our view, this is a healthy initial response. The Bible makes it clear that God is outraged by evil. He hates the destructive effects of evil in the world. He is not a cynical God who blithely brushes aside the world's lack of love as if it didn't matter. In the same way, when our initial response to an injury is anger, the pain and outrage is an acknowledgment that there has been a moral injustice. It shows that we are morally sensitive.

But from that point on we are called to follow Jesus and his command to forgive, as he depicted in the story of the king and the servant. Soon we encounter a barrage of emotions and intellectual conflict. The angry response to injustice can twist into prideful bitterness, which in turn can dictate our decisions and shape our behavior. We begin to long for more than fair redress. What we really want is to *defeat* the person who subjected us to so much pain, and to gain a position of moral superiority.

On an even more subtle level, it is common for people to find self-validation in the pain and anger they feel. For example, we have a close friend who described how for more than a year she struggled to forgive a person who had repeatedly made her feel put down and unimportant during their conversations. Our friend always felt demeaned and controlled by the other person. The painful feelings were so strong that she often didn't sleep at night. She talked about the situation to the person who was hurting her, but even those conversations seemed to make matters worse.

As a follower of Christ, our friend knew that she needed to forgive the person who was hurting her. And she sincerely wanted to be free from the feelings of anger and pain. So every morning she would wake up and pray about it. But the painful feelings did not subside. After much prayer, she realized that she had been clinging to her grief rather than forgiving because, in a subtle and subconscious way, it bolstered her sense of moral superiority.

She came to a point of true freedom when she stopped clinging to her pain. She renounced her protest and submitted her demands into the hands of God. And from that point on she felt the freedom that comes from true forgiveness.

Most of this long process happened privately between our friend and God. It was an invisible series of steps that involved prayer and God's Word. Her dialogue with God gradually resulted not only in her personal freedom—the freedom to be the person she was called by God to be—but it also brought about increased maturity and character.

Her story helps us understand that forgiveness is a step-by-step process rather than a one-time event. In the small conflicts, forgiveness might come easily and quickly. But when there are more difficult matters to resolve, it may be that we have to progress toward forgiveness a step at a time.

The process of forgiveness hinges on humility, which we discussed in the last chapter. Over the past couple years, I (Jim) have been reading the Scriptures with a good friend, Miguel. Not long ago, we explored a key sentence in Paul's letter to the Romans: "This righteousness from God comes through faith in Jesus Christ to all who believe."[8] The word *righteousness* in this sentence means "perfection." Paul is saying that this perfect righteousness becomes ours not by personal merit but as a gift from God, through faith, as we believe in Jesus Christ. Period! There is nothing more to add or do. This is the lens God looks through as he views us. He sees us in light of the perfection of his Son rather than the fact of our sinfulness. And as a result, he *declares us to be perfect*. So "there is now no condemnation for those who are in Christ Jesus."[9]

A few days after we read this together, Miguel read another passage in the book of Ephesians, which says that "husbands ought to love their wives as their own bodies. . . . He feeds and cares for it, just as Christ does the church."[10] Reflecting on these two Scriptures, Miguel concluded that because he was free from God's condemnation, he should also treat the people in his life in the same way, with equal grace and mercy. As he thought about how he tended to put people down and leave them feeling judged, he decided that such behavior had to end.

Miguel's experience of God's forgiveness led him to a position of humility. He recognized that he had done nothing to deserve the righteousness that God had given him. From this position of humility before God, he understood his need to change the way he related to others.

This is the powerful implication of Jesus' story about the king who forgave his servant. When we comprehend the gravity of our moral condition and the gift of God's grace, how can we not forgive the offenses that others have committed against us?

FROM FORGIVENESS TO RECONCILIATION

As people work through the process of forgiveness, it is important to understand that forgiveness is *not* reconciliation. Forgiveness is limited to the process of canceling the debt caused by moral failure, releasing someone from what is owed to you. Forgiveness is necessary for reconciliation to occur, of course, but we are not required to pursue reconciliation in all situations. And, because reconciliation depends on the response of both people involved, a positive result is always beyond the control of a forgiving person who might seek to renew the relationship.

Many terrible offenses are caused by people with whom we have never had a relationship. Consider the case of a relative who is murdered by a stranger. In this case, the family is called by God to forgive the criminal, but they are not required to establish a relationship with the person.

But in most circumstances, the people we offend and who offend us are friends, relatives, colleagues, and neighbors. In these cases, the issue of reconciliation becomes more important. Discernment is needed to know how to respond in each situation. We can't discuss every possible scenario, but there are some guiding principles.

Let's imagine a common situation in which a marriage has been broken by a wife's adultery. Assuming that the husband has moved through the process of forgiveness, the natural next question is whether he should pursue the restoration of his relationship or whether he should end the matter in divorce. Such a decision is bound to be saturated with competing emotions and intellectual questions. And it must be a mutual decision. As we have said, reconciliation requires the participation of both people.

Jesus said that divorce is sometimes necessary and that adultery is a morally justified reason for it.[11] So in this case there is no moral requirement for the husband to pursue reconciliation. He is free to attempt to restore his marriage if he should so desire, but he would need great courage and wisdom to risk his heart again. The wife's lack of integrity would have caused a breakdown in the couple's foundational trust. To pursue reconciliation, one of the greatest obstacles to restored intimacy is the challenge of restoring the confidence that was once inherent in the relationship.

God does not ask the offended person to simply step back into the line of fire. His command that we forgive one another does not mean that we must set ourselves up for further abuse. He values our lives. In cases where there has been serious breach of trust, the offended person should cautiously consider whether or not the offender is making *true life changes*, not just verbal apologies. To build trust, one must demonstrate integrity in attitude and action. Words are not sufficient.

It is sometimes better not to pursue a restored relationship. On several occasions, Jesus turned away from people because he knew that their hearts were hard. He did not entrust himself to everyone even though he offered them forgiveness.[12] Many people overlook the fact that God at one point in history decided to give the people of Israel a "writ of divorce." The prophet Jeremiah, writing a lament from the heart of God, describes how God had loved and cared for his people as a husband cares for his wife. But they continued to pursue other gods. Jeremiah captures the conflict within God, the tension between his longing for reconciliation and their hardened hearts toward him:

> If a husband divorces his wife,
>   And she goes from him
>   And belongs to another man,
>   Will he still return to her?
>
> . . . .
>
> "Return, faithless Israel," declares the LORD;
>   "I will not look upon you in anger.
>   For I am gracious," declares the LORD;
>   "I will not be angry forever.
> Only acknowledge your iniquity,
>   That you have transgressed against the LORD your
>   God."[13]

As we have been saying throughout this book, God's greatest desire is for us to experience a profound and permanent unity with him and with one another. Reconciliation is the highest, most beautiful ambition of God. God's heart is demonstrated in stories like the return of the prodigal son in Luke 15. Therefore, reconciliation should also be our highest aspiration and goal. But God recognizes that, due to the hardness of the human heart, there are circumstances when reconciliation is not possible or even advisable. Forgiveness opens the door to reconciliation, but it is a door that we need not always pass through.

However, even in cases where reconciliation is not possible, it is crucial that we forgive one another. Jesus promised a rich and rewarding life to those who follow him in forgiveness.

THE AMAZING BENEFITS OF FORGIVENESS

When my wife and I (Jim) first started dating, we experienced a wonderful season of mutual discovery. I found myself telling her everything that was going on in my mind, and she would do the same. Our love and confidence blossomed in a judgment-free atmosphere. This spirit carried into the early months of our marriage. I was still in school, and we were broke, but the financial struggle didn't seem to matter. We started out in a little house with no furniture. Life was beautiful.

But as we lived together day-to-day in close proximity, I began to notice things about her that bothered me. She would drop the soap every time she took a shower. And she would leave the newspaper spread out after she had finished reading it. I didn't say anything because everything was so perfect. But I began taking mental notes about her little flaws.

Then one day an argument flared up. I don't remember what caused the argument, but I remember bringing up her habits of dropping the soap and leaving the newspaper scattered around. During the argument, I discovered she, too, had been taking similar notes about my defects. It bothered her that I would leave my jeans draped over a chair and my dirty underwear on the floor.

The argument didn't last long, and we quickly made up. But our bubble had popped. We realized we had begun to judge each other. And the judgment list included more serious indictments which marred our harmony. Somehow, the same list of judgments would find their way into every argument we had, no matter what the issue happened to be.

We were robbing each other of life and freedom. One day, as I was reading Paul's letter to the Ephesians, a phrase that gave us what we needed jumped off the page: "Be kind and compassionate to one another, forgiving each other, just as in Christ God forgave you."[14]

I learned from Paul's words that we had a *permanent* responsibility to forgive one another every day and in every detail of life. Forgiveness applied as much to our biting little judgments against one another as to the major offenses. I realized that the judgments were in fact my problem, not hers. I was developing some bad mental habits that were feeding these judgments. When something would happen, I would mentally add it to the list. *There she goes again*, I would think. In this way I was constantly reinforcing my judgments. I realized I had to let that habit go, just reject it whenever it came into my mind. And I knew nobody else could do that for me.

It was clear to me that forgiveness was my responsibility. That obligation would only end when God stopped forgiving us—which would be never. It took a while, but soon we began to smell the fresh air of freedom and acceptance blowing through our relationship again.

Judgments are insidious. As Paul Tournier wrote, judgment "insinuates itself surreptitiously, unnoticed, and secretly eats away at the structure of an apparently happy marriage."[15] Like weeds in a garden, judgments are bound to grow up in any relationship. Where forgiveness is lacking, judgment takes over and chokes the life out of it. Forgiveness replaces judgments with freedom. It tears out the weeds and restores the beauty.

This is the greatest reward of forgiveness. It preserves unity and intimacy—even in the small interactions of our lives together. It creates an environment of freedom and safety, a relational landscape that allows people to share their deepest struggles and to know they will be accepted. When forgiveness fills the room, judgments and accusations are forced out.

The second benefit of forgiveness seems illogical. Forgiveness is a deliberate choice to set another person free from judgment and condemnation. It is easy, therefore, to understand why the *forgiven* person would experience freedom. But surprisingly, forgiveness also produces freedom in the life of the person who forgives.

In my interactions with people, I (David) have found that people who truly forgive those who have offended them feel a huge sense of relief. They often say things like "a heavy weight has been lifted off of me."

This is a mysterious truth, because the person who forgives continues to hold the weight of the loss. When we release someone from a debt, we no longer demand repayment and therefore must be content with assuming the loss. The burden stays on our shoulders. So why does the act of forgiveness so universally generate inner freedom?

The immediate and natural inclination is to protest against those who hurt us. But this all-consuming demand for justice ends up controlling our thoughts and actions—sometimes leading to terrible consequences. When a person forgives, he stops the protest. He moves beyond the demand for justice and into a broader reason for living. He finds the freedom to be himself again and to live for higher purposes. Ending the tiresome march against injustice, he not only gives the perpetrator a new chance at life but he himself experiences the freedom to live a noble life. Without forgiveness, bitterness controls the person and chains him to the offender.

There is a man who, at a young age, found out that his father had been unfaithful to his mother. Everything he believed about his father was shattered. There had been so much deceit that he no longer knew what to believe about his dad. The rage and hurt that boiled inside him was almost uncontainable.

Over the years he responded by making a conscious decision to never be like his father. He developed an unassailable devotion to his mother and sister. And he promised himself that he would always be faithful to his wife when the opportunity for marriage came his way. Underneath these promises, however, was unresolved anger.

The man did get married after a sincere and passionate courtship. But in the early years of marriage, several disconcerting signs emerged. A low-grade coldness developed in the relationship. Conflicts increased in frequency and intensity. Gradually, the man began to distance himself emotionally from his wife, and then the threat of divorce raised its ugly head.

Underneath his commitment was a distorted motivation. An essential aspect of his motivation was to *not* be like his father rather than to demonstrate love, humility, and integrity to his wife. As conflict developed, he was intolerant of additional wounds, as he had never resolved the bitterness with his father. He began to justify leaving his wife by declaring he would not be like his mother and put up with this. And ultimately, in the highest irony, he left his wife even as she pled with him to stay. He had reproduced his father's sin.

All of these problems stemmed from a lack of forgiveness. For years, the man didn't fully realize how much these feelings had ruled his decisions and shaped his character. Forgiveness would have provided him with the freedom to be the person God designed him to be rather than spend his life trying not to be someone else.

Therefore, when Jesus commanded his followers to forgive one another—not just once or twice but perpetually and in all situations—he provided us with a principle that seems unfair but that in reality protects our inner being. It's easy to understand why our wounded souls would so fervently demand repair. But who would have imagined that the repair would come from voluntarily relinquishing the demand?

Forgiveness opens the door to yet another relational treasure, only this time the benefits extend far beyond the self: Forgiveness not only brings about personal freedom, *it stops the cycle of evil*. By accepting the loss imposed on us by an offender and then forgiving that person, we are refusing to enter into the destructive cycle of revenge.

This, too, is the model of Jesus. He knew that forgiveness was the only way to overcome evil and to provide the necessary conditions for a more beautiful story. Miroslav Volf wrote:

> [Jesus] refused to be sucked into the automatism of revenge, but sought to overcome evil by doing good—even at the cost of his life. . . . Jesus' kind of option for nonviolence had nothing to do with the self-abnegation in which I completely place myself at the disposal of others to do with me as they please; it had much to do with the kind of self-assertion in which I refuse to be ensnared in the dumb redoubling of my enemies' violent gestures and be reshaped into their mirror image.[16]

In Christ, forgiveness becomes not just a pointless act of personal suffering, but the transforming force that creates new possibilities for relationships that are restored to God's original design.

God's passion is to restore deeply flawed people who live broken lives to a life of relational joy and purpose. Forgiveness is the bridge between the world as it is and the world that will be. Forgiveness is the surgery of redemption. It is not passive but proactive and dynamic. And to the extent that we forgive one another, we are working with God to redeem the world around us. The choice to forgive is a choice to contribute to God's venerable purpose in the world. Through forgiveness we embrace the meaning of life.

FOUNDATIONAL TRUST

Behind every decision to forgive a person who has wounded you—no matter how severely—is an important question: "What about me and my needs?" We resist forgiveness because we fear that our own needs will not be met. Forgiveness, we think, will minimize the horror of the offense, lessening the importance of our suffering. And it seems as though it will diminish the value of our identities. Our intense drive to impose justice on those who offend us is a fight for our own dignity as human beings.

These valid concerns are especially prominent when serious offenses such as marital infidelity, sexual abuse, or violence are involved. Forgiveness can make people feel as though what has happened to them does not matter, that the horrible aggression will be left unaddressed. They wonder if the years of pain will matter to God. Deeper still, they worry that perhaps *they* don't matter to God.

Therefore, to forgive others we need assurance that we are valuable to God, that our pain means something to him, and that he will take up our case. And, thankfully, the Scriptures are filled with these promises.

First, it is crucial to realize that *forgiveness does not reduce the weight of the offense*. Forgiveness is not the same thing as an acquittal. A legal acquittal is when a judge rules that the accused never committed the crime. But forgiveness is by definition an acknowledgement of the crime and a proclamation of its severity. Forgiveness does not void the crime, it only releases the criminal from the deserved penalty.

Again, we see this when Jesus died on the cross. The fact that he had to suffer such brutality on our behalf was a bold statement about the immensity of our guilt before God—the severity of sin. The forgiveness of Jesus is a loud pronouncement of humanity's moral guilt. For this reason, accepting God's forgiveness provided through Christ is often a difficult step; it requires us to admit the severity of our moral failures.

We also need to know that God will not forget our losses. The Scriptures clearly state that every man is "destined to die once, and after that to face judgment."[17] But for those who have received the forgiveness of God bought with the life of his son, judgment does not lead to condemnation but rather to the embrace of God.[18] For those who refuse to receive the forgiveness of God, there is no option left except to receive the due consequence of their injustice.

One way or another, we can be sure that there will be ultimate justice from God. Either the justice of God for moral failure will have been absorbed by Jesus, or it will be absorbed by the person who rejects his offer of forgiveness.

So, when we forgive someone, God does not minimize what has happened to us. But when we forgive, we end our attempt to be the judge and jury, and we give that responsibility into the sovereign hands of God. Paul, writing in Romans, said, "Never take your own revenge, beloved, but leave room for the wrath of God, for it is written, 'VENGEANCE IS MINE, I WILL REPAY,' says the Lord."[19] In other words, in matters of judgment you are not in the loop.

This was the insight that allowed me (David) to forgive my friend's murderer. Once I relinquished the judgment to God and trusted he would do what was right, I was free to forgive.

"God will judge, not because God gives people what they deserve, but because some people refuse to receive what no one deserves," wrote Volf. "If evildoers experience God's terror, it will not be because they have done evil, but because they have resisted to the end the powerful lure of the open arms of the crucified Messiah."[20]

Therefore, true forgiveness requires us to entrust all of our pain, our anger, our longing for justice, our personal needs, our fears, and our future into the hands of God. We have to believe that the sovereign God will provide for our physical losses and restore our souls. We must trust that he will—in this life or the next—restore our losses and balance the scales. Most importantly, we must trust that the sovereignty of God will not allow us to suffer in vain, that our lives will be meaningful even as we live in the wreckage of this world, and that we can be his instruments for building a more beautiful world that reflects his original design.

Even in this trust, Jesus shows us the way. Peter wrote, "When they hurled their insults at him, he did not retaliate; when he suffered, he made no threats. Instead, he *entrusted* himself to him who judges justly."[21]

Finally, there will be a day when forgiveness and reconciliation will be victorious over all pain and division. The book of Revelation states, "Now the dwelling of God is with men, and he will live with them. . . . He will wipe every tear from their eyes. There will be no more death or mourning or crying or pain, for the old order of things has passed away."[22]

In the next chapter we will show how all four essential character traits—integrity, love, humility, and forgiveness—must work together in order for our relationships to thrive. They are an inseparable whole. In order to demonstrate this we have employed a hypothetical case study that will show the practical implications as well as the internal tensions of the four essentials as they unfold in our relationships.

QUESTIONS FOR DISCUSSION

1. What is forgiveness?
2. Why is forgiveness essential to any healthy relationship? What happens in a relationship where forgiveness is absent?
3. What does forgiveness accomplish in a relationship?
4. When do you know that you have truly forgiven someone?
5. What is our basis for forgiving others? What makes it just?
6. Have you experienced situations where forgiveness seems complicated and/or you have felt resistance to forgive? Can you describe what makes it complicated or difficult?

Chapter 9

MADELYN AND ALLAN

In this fictional account of an all-too-common relationship, we display the inseparable unity of integrity, love, humility, and forgiveness. Although they are essential for intimacy, they provoke dilemmas and tensions in our souls that often cause us to hide from the relationships we most need and desire. And they inevitably reveal our innate weaknesses and thus our need for God.

M adelyn sat alone at her kitchen table. A shaft of sunlight illuminated waves of steam that swirled above her teacup. Today was her fifty-fifth birthday, and her hair was now mostly gray. Last year she had decided to stop adding color to it. Even though hair treatments made her look younger, she felt that at her age she had the right to be true to herself. There was no need to pretend anymore, and in this she found pleasurable freedom.

145

As she sipped her tea, Allan, her husband of thirty years, played chess online, which is what he did whenever he had the chance. From where she sat, she could see the back of his bald head and the faint glow of the computer shimmering around his shoulders, like the light of the sun when in full eclipse. It was late afternoon, and he had been sitting in the same place for the past three hours.

He had barely talked to her all day. There had been no mention of her birthday. During lunch they discussed how Allan might need to find a second job. His boss at the utility company, where he had worked as an electrical technician for the past thirteen years, refused to give him a raise. And having been depleted to put all three kids through college, their savings was almost gone. Even with Madelyn working as a teacher, Allan fretted constantly about his retirement.

Madelyn had left her teaching career when their first son was born. Teaching was a joy, but she never felt that staying home to raise the kids had been a sacrifice. And even now she felt blessed to have had so much time with her children. As the kids became more independent, she had arranged to do some occasional substitute teaching at the neighborhood school and had attended conferences in order to stay in tune with the pedagogical trends. But for the most part, her married life had consisted of caring for her children. She still believed this had been a good investment.

Madelyn worried that her kids might not visit her today as she added more tea to her flowered porcelain cup. The teacup had first belonged to her great-grandmother. It became a family heirloom and was passed down to Madelyn. Her mother had presented it to her the night before she married Allan. The moment her mother placed the antique in her hand, its smooth surface and elegant lines connected her to the strong, beautiful women in her family tree. It was as if she had received a runner's baton, a symbol of her heritage and her responsibility to live well. In that cherished moment with her mother, she remembered having a deep longing to build a new life and identity with Allan, to write a story with him that would be as beautiful as her own mother's had been.

But now the teacup seemed like a symbol of lament. It reminded Madelyn of all her unfulfilled hopes. She wrapped both hands around the cup to warm them, hoping it would comfort her, but instead her mind filled with anxious thoughts. Her life had turned into a cul-de-sac. She felt trapped, alone, and afraid.

Even before her kids moved away, Madelyn had been planning a strategy to start teaching full-time again, mostly because living with Allan had become like living with a brick wall. Teaching full-time might restore some adventure to her life and even prepare her financially in the event that Allan decided to leave her. And if he didn't, teaching would be a good way to distance herself from him and give her contact with other people. Indeed, the school had become a respite from home, a place where she was respected, and a place where she felt like she was making a difference. But, inside, she knew that work had not compensated for the emptiness of her life with Allan.

Her thoughts drifted back to the years when the kids needed her constant service. She missed those days. As each grown child moved away, the distance between her and Allan became increasingly apparent. Without the kids to fill the empty space between them, it seemed that they orbited one another, silently, without ever connecting, like cold planets.

Madelyn longed for her children to be home, especially today. She ached for companionship. But if they didn't come, she would understand. They were busy professionals, and she knew about the intense demands on people starting new careers. Moreover, she knew that home didn't feel the same as it did in the early years of their lives. She understood why they didn't want to visit anymore. The emptiness of the home was difficult for everyone to endure.

Allan interrupted her thoughts. "Madelyn, I need to pay the bills. Do you know where I put them?"

Madelyn walked over to a kitchen drawer and pulled out a stack of envelopes. She stepped over to the computer and handed the bills to Allan, who had switched from the chess website to his bank account.

"Are we going to be able to pay the bills this month without taking from savings?" Madelyn asked cautiously.

"What is that supposed to mean?" he replied, without looking at her.

"I'm just wondering where we stand this month. That's all."

"Look," he said, turning toward her in his desk chair. "You think you can do a better job with money, but I only see you spending too much on stuff we don't need. I'll handle the money. Why don't you quit complaining?"

"What do mean, 'stuff we don't need?'" Madelyn retorted. "I hand my salary over to you every month and get no appreciation. Then I spend Saturday mornings clipping coupons to save money on toilet paper and cereal. If you think you can do better at shopping, be my guest."

"By the look of this house, you need to clip more coupons for cleaning supplies," he said as he spun back around in the chair and faced his computer. There were a few seconds of angry silence. Then Allan spitefully ran his index finger across the top of his desk, leaving a clean swipe in the middle of a thin layer of dust.

"If you'd ever get up from the computer, I might be able to clean your desk," she said, walking away. Allan didn't reply.

Madelyn stalked to the front door of the house and stepped

into the cool autumn air. She felt like walking somewhere far from home, but there was nowhere to go.

When the screen door slammed behind her, Madelyn heard Allan strike his fist on the desk and mutter, "What the hell is her problem! It's not like I am a lazy drunk. I have worked hard for thirty years. I'm sick of not being respected. No matter what I do, it's never enough."

She sat down on the porch step and watched the red and gold maple leaves blowing in the wind. The warm colors of the setting sun softened her anger, but that just uncapped her underlying sadness. Tears filled her eyes.

She wondered how life with Allan had become so unbearable. It was as if the husband she loved had disappeared. He had locked her out of everything—his thoughts, his heart, his bank account. Even his computer had a private password that kept her from entering. And all this hiding occasionally made her wonder what or who he was trying to hide from her. To think such thoughts without evidence made her feel guilty. Allan probably wouldn't go that far, but neither could she deny her feelings of distrust.

Madelyn still hoped to restore her marriage. But with every harsh conversation, with every reckless accusation, the emotional love in her heart grew increasingly faint. Today, as the leaves fell to the ground, she feared that she might not be able to recover her feelings for the man she once so passionately loved. For her, the relationship was starting to feel like jury duty. She stayed in it mostly because she was afraid of what might happen to her if she left, but also because she had made a promise to remain faithful to Allan until the end of her life or his. But the chasm between them seemed as though it would be impossible to bridge.

The sunlight had dropped below the branches of the trees and directly illuminated Madelyn's face with warm hues. Her thoughts drifted back to the early years with Allan. Those were beautiful times. They would sit on their cheap sofa with a candle on the coffee table, pour a little red wine, and listen to soft jazz in the dark. Though they said nothing, Madelyn remembered resting her head on his shoulder and feeling the deep bond of their souls.

That memory reminded her of the days when Allan *pursued* her with all his heart and when he would share his deepest thoughts and feelings with her. They had the freedom to express any failure without fear. He was an open book. She knew his inner struggles—with work, with fatherhood, with his friends. Even the exhausting job of raising small children didn't diminish the peace between them. Peace was the air they breathed.

Even in moments of conflict, Madelyn remembered that their relationship seemed as though it would never falter. In their second year of marriage, when Allan received an end-of-the-year bonus, Madelyn had impulsively bought an expensive vacation package for them, not knowing that Allan had sent a large sum to pay off his college loan. They fought about it briefly and then spent a couple of silent hours in front of the TV, sulking. But then Madelyn realized that she had wrongly spent the money. She went to Allan and asked for forgiveness. And Allan had forgiven her completely. He also had apologized for not communicating with her about his plans to pay off the loan. They agreed to do a better job of talking about money. It was as if nothing could break them apart.

She also remembered that Allan's little flaws didn't bother her then as they did today. He ate his meals too fast, and his table manners were unrefined. His closets were always in disarray. He tended to get lost when they traveled by car. She wished that he would shave more often and be more concerned for his clothing styles. She didn't like these aspects of Allan back then, but those traits were overshadowed by his work ethic, his strong leadership in the family, his love for people, and his dedication to meeting her own needs every day. After a long day of work, he always came home looking for ways to help in the kitchen and to play with the kids. She knew him, and she could trust him.

Perhaps more importantly, the Allan she had married accepted her despite her own shortfalls. Madelyn was fully aware of her failures. But in those days, it seemed that Allan didn't notice any of them. He only saw her positive qualities. She remembered always feeling amazed that he would love her and find her physically beautiful. He never criticized her. Although he was not overly romantic, he would often touch her affectionately through the course of the day — little reassurances that he loved her. She never felt like she had to do anything to prove herself around Allan.

As the breeze whirled the fallen leaves in circles, Madelyn remembered the year that the tornado had ripped through town. Their children were young, asleep in their beds. It was 5:00 a.m. when Allan heard the warning siren peal. He then gently carried each of the children to the basement. They were frightened and confused, but he calmed them by setting up his camping tent and rolling out the sleeping bags inside it, dissipating the fear in their hearts with fun and adventure. By the light of a flashlight, they had all hunkered down in the tent and read stories about Pippi Longstocking, that strong, crazy girl who could toss a horse with one hand. By reading that story, he made them feel stronger than the tornado. Then, when the all-clear siren blew, Allan took the truck and went through the town helping people whose homes had been damaged. When he came home that night, tired and dirty, he was the children's hero. He was Madelyn's hero.

This was the Allan that Madelyn married: an honest, hardworking, loving, good man. The whole town knew him this way too. She would walk down the street, feeling proud to be married to Allan.

All that seemed like another life now, maybe a dream. Allan's slow drift away from her seemed to have been triggered when he had lost his job, about fifteen years ago. That was a hard blow to Allan, who loved to work. He had been let go unfairly and coldly, not because he had done anything wrong but because of company politics. The whole affair left him feeling unappreciated, disrespected, and demoralized. His emotional state deteriorated after eighteen months of unemployment. Without his work, Allan seemed to have lost his sense of manhood and personal value. Even though he was now gainfully employed, his work was not as satisfying as his old profession. It paid most of the bills, but work was no longer an expression of Allan's personality. At fifty-eight years of age, he didn't believe there was much chance of making a career change. The financial limitations only fueled his frustrations more.

Madelyn looked across the street and saw her neighbors, Dave and Ilene McCarly, working in their flower garden, preparing it for the onset of winter, trimming back the roses and raking leaves. In their late seventies, they could still handle some manual labor, and gardening was what they most enjoyed. They had lived in the red brick house for about thirty-five years. On some weekends, their house bustled with a little flock of grandchildren playing hide-and-seek in the front yard.

Madelyn had known the McCarlys for a long time. Her children had often played at their house when she had errands to run, and Ilene would use this as an excuse to serve Madelyn tea and have a long chat when she came to pick up her kids. They usually talked about raising children, conversations that often gave Madelyn, a less experienced mother, the guidance that she needed.

The vision of this elderly couple working in the garden

together—obviously still in love—filled Madelyn with a mixture of longing and pain. The sight stirred Madelyn's hope, but also her fears. She wanted the beauty they had between them. But after all she had suffered, she was afraid to hope again.

At this moment, hope conquered her fear. She stood up and walked across the street. As she got closer to the McCarlys, they looked up from the plants and waved. Madelyn stepped into their yard, hoping they wouldn't notice that she had been crying.

Dave and Ilene stood up from their gardening stools and took off their dirty gloves. They and Madelyn talked a little about the garden, the beautiful autumn day, and whether or not the winter would be as cold as the previous one. Ilene asked,. "Madelyn, isn't today your birthday?" That someone had remembered her birthday caused Madelyn, already emotionally fragile, to cry. Ilene put her arm around the tearful woman and all three went into the house.

Madelyn sat on the sofa, a tissue in hand, while the McCarlys listened attentively to her story. She told them everything she had been experiencing at home, about how Allan had become increasingly distant from her. Years of pain spilled out of Madelyn's heart in a tone of mixed sadness and anger.

"I'm wasting my life with him," Madelyn finally said, her perfunctory conclusion to a long outpouring. It was all on the table, her neighbor's table. And now Madelyn felt a wave of guilt for having spent so much of the McCarlys' time and for having levied so many accusations against Allan. She apologized and looked down to her lap.

After a few seconds of silence, Madelyn said: "I don't know what to do. I have tried everything I know to salvage this mess, but I am out of ideas and out of energy. I'm afraid that I am running out of love. But something in me hopes for what you two still have. I saw you in the garden today and . . ." Madelyn again couldn't control her tears.

"Madelyn," said Dave. "We've had our difficulties through the years."

"You obviously have done something right," Madelyn replied.

"We're not a perfect family. Ilene got so mad at me once that I had to spend three days in a hotel room," he said. "But we have managed to hold strong through the difficulties of life, and today we are still happy together."

"So how have you done that?" Madelyn asked.

"That's a big question, but I guarantee you it isn't because we are different or better than you and Allan. It has taken something beyond our own capacity. I don't want to impose anything on you, but for us it all comes down to the fact that we have given room for God to work in our lives."

Madelyn looked at Dave. She had known that they read the Bible. Ilene had mentioned a little about her belief in God, but Madelyn had never taken the subject to a deeper level. The Bible was always sitting on a table when she visited them over the years, but she never knew them to attend church. She always thought that maybe they were just nominally religious. That God was so important in their lives surprised her.

"Madelyn, do you think your marriage can be saved?" Ilene asked.

Madelyn sat quietly and thought about how to answer. There was still a small flame of love for Allan in her heart, but the anger, frustration, and emotional fatigue seemed overwhelming. "I don't think I can," she said.

"You didn't answer my question, Madelyn."

"Yes, I guess I would like my marriage to be saved," she said. "But I've tried everything I know, and he doesn't change. If anything, he seems to get worse."

"I know you are feeling a lot of confusion and pain, but I think it will have to start with you, not Allan," Dave said. "You can't control what he will do or won't do. But you can decide what to do in your own heart. The first question is: Do you really want to try and save your marriage? If you do, then I believe there is hope. We have seen this in our own lives."

"To be honest," said Madelyn, "it's not that I don't want to restore my relationship with Allan; it's that I am afraid of trying again and getting hurt. I don't know if I can risk my heart again."

"That is certainly understandable," said Ilene. "You need to be careful with yourself. But the only way toward restoration is to overcome your natural fears. When it comes to our own fears, it has helped us to trust God."

Dave walked into his office and returned with a brown Bible. He sat down and began to search through its pages with his old, distinguished fingers. Madelyn noticed that the gold wedding band on his left hand showed the signs of its age.

"I hope you don't mind, but I'd like to read something for you to think about," he said. "Paul wrote these words: 'Be kind and compassionate to one another, forgiving each other, just as in Christ God forgave you. Be imitators of God . . . and live a life of love, just as Christ loved us and gave himself up for us.'[1] What do you think of that idea, Madelyn?"

"Well, it sounds nice," she replied, "but Paul didn't have to live with Allan."

"No, but Paul wrote those words to a group of people who struggled with many serious relational problems like yours," Dave said. "What's interesting about this is that Paul didn't tell his friends to live like Jesus only when other people were nice to them. He made it clear that living a life of love is always the right thing to do, no matter how other people respond to our efforts. In fact, Jesus himself loved and forgave people even though almost everyone hated him. The point is, Madelyn, it doesn't start with Allan. It starts with you and your own relationship with God."

"It doesn't seem fair," said Madelyn. "He has wrecked my life, and now it's my responsibility to forgive him and love him?"

"Someone has to break the downward spiral," said Ilene. "It's not necessarily fair, and it's risky, but it is the path to healing and wholeness. If you do that, there is a great chance that Allan will respond. Love and forgiveness are very powerful."

The room had grown dim. Dave got up to turn on a lamp by the sofa. Madelyn realized that it was time to make dinner.

"I need some time to think about this," Madelyn said, standing up from the sofa. She thanked her neighbors, hugged each one tightly, and said goodbye. As she walked back home, her thoughts shifted to the job ahead—making chili and enduring another silent meal with Allan. She had hoped to feel more comforted by her time with the McCarlys. What they had said seemed true, but it was not a truth she wanted to hear.

It is easy to see from this all-too-common story that the four essentials modeled by Jesus were prominent in the early days of Madelyn's marriage with Allan. His integrity in all areas of life enabled Madelyn to trust him. He actively loved his wife and children and nurtured each person's deepest inner needs. Despite their financial struggles, love made them rich. Humility also ran through their relationship, helping them to admit wrongs and to forgive one another. This humility protected them from selfish attitudes. It made Allan a servant in his home. The spirit of forgiveness they shared enabled them to survive the natural conflicts of life. Forgiveness prevented them from judging one another.

Later in the story, the absence of the four essentials led Madelyn and Allan to tragic levels of relational breakdown.

They relate to one another purely on the basis of reflexive, emotional, self-centered responses and motivations. Allan hides the financial picture from Madelyn and makes major decisions without her involvement. A general lack of integrity has eroded the trust they once enjoyed. They have no pleasure in the presence of the other; what remains is an environment of bitterness and anger. They keep a list of wrongs against one another, tossing the evidence in the face of the other when it is useful for self-justification. Verbal criticism is their way of taking revenge. All these problems lock them into an emotionally exhausting vicious cycle.

Now Madelyn finds herself at a crossroads. The choice she faces is either to follow her natural instincts and take flight, or to pursue a renewed relationship. Her emotions tell her to give up. The long struggle has drained the life and willpower from her soul. Moreover, there is no guarantee that loving and forgiving Allan will bring about change in his heart. The cost to her seems high, and positive returns don't seem probable.

These legitimate concerns, however, operate in direct opposition to her inner longings for a restored relationship with Allan. She continues to feel the "image of God" in her soul that longs for intimacy, security, and love. This is why the sight of her neighbors working in the garden touched her heart so strongly. She feels that if she loses the relationship, she will have lost the man of her life and an entire segment of her personal history. The thought of walking away from all that feels like amputating part of her soul.

Where does she go from here?

SEEKING HELP

Most people today, if they found themselves in such confusion and distress, would seek out professional help from a therapist or counselor. And this can be a good first step. A therapist can provide two important resources: a safe environment for self-disclosure and professional guidance.

Many people lack a relationship in which they can share the deep struggles of life. One reason for this is that they are ashamed and fearful of being judged. To fully expose one's heart is intimidating, especially in our competitive culture. For many, a therapist is the only person safe enough with whom to expose these hidden realities. Most people understand that therapy is not about condemnation.

People also go to therapists hoping to find truthful feedback about their circumstances, even about personal failures and character flaws. Contrary to the "I'm okay, you're okay" theories, people know they are *not* okay and don't mind hearing it—as long as the therapist cares about them. As I (David) have learned over the past twenty years, people don't want platitudes that ignore failure. They want me to be accurate but also gentle and hopeful. And a good therapist will offer the person nonjudgmental but truthful counsel.

That people seek therapy as a source of guidance and wisdom is a tendency that has been evident since psychotherapy's beginnings. Mark Edmundson, author of a book about Sigmund Freud, says that Freud's patients "wanted perfect love, and even more fervently, it seems, they wanted perfect truth. . . . Patients saw Freud as an all-knowing figure who had the wisdom to solve all their problems and make them genuinely happy and whole."[2]

Psychotherapy is a highly diverse field rooted in a multitude of philosophies. Each approach operates with a different view of human nature and will therefore offer divergent solutions to the problems people face. This means that there is no guarantee that the client will find the wisdom and guidance he or she seeks.

But a good therapist can be very effective in helping people develop a "map" of themselves and their circumstances, putting the puzzle pieces in a manageable order. The process of therapy can assist people as they talk through one "rough draft after another" of their personal map.[3]

To create this map, the therapist and client develop a thorough description of the symptoms, the significant events, the important people, and even physical concerns. Moreover, therapy usually helps clients recognize their core beliefs about themselves and the world, showing them how those beliefs affect their values, behavior, and emotions.

While therapy can provide a safe environment and educated guidance, the therapeutic process has several significant limits when it comes to bringing about true character transformation. Let's imagine that a person has received an accurate map of the problems and has received a perfect set of solutions to resolve these difficulties. Would that suffice? Would self-knowledge plus a suitable treatment method automatically solve the difficulties?

John Gottman, who is a leading authority in marital research, has done a brilliant job of diagnosing, through empirical observation of couples over two decades, the factors that destroy marriages. Although he doesn't use the same terms we use in this book, his conclusions are consistent with the four essentials found in the Bible.

In his book *Why Marriages Succeed or Fail*, Gottman also provides some excellent techniques to improve relationships. For example, if the couple is too critical of one another, they should "learn to state your grievances and complaints in a manner that your spouse will not take as a personal attack."[4] If there is contempt in the marriage, the partners should "replace that habit with the expression of genuine validation and admiration."[5] If a husband finds himself being too defensive and overwhelmed by a partner's complaints, he should "master ways to speak and listen non-defensively."[6] This is done by "choosing to have a positive mindset about your spouse and to reintroduce praise and admiration into your relationship. . . . You need to become the architect of your thoughts."[7]

But here is the core limitation of therapy. Consider the condition of Madelyn's heart, mind, and thoughts. Therapy would assume that Madelyn *naturally* has the character, the inner desire, the will, and the emotional resources needed to apply the prescribed remedies. It's assumed that with the right information Madelyn will be able to pull herself up by her own bootstraps. In reality, we are often so offended, hurt, fearful, and angry that we lack the basic inner desire to even think about implementing a therapist's recommendations.

The therapeutic process can be a very helpful and important element of relational and personal healing. But, in general, when the client leaves the therapist's office, he or she must fight the battles alone with nothing more than his or her inner resources. In our secular therapeutic society, both the client and the therapist assume that the client naturally has the character traits needed to carry out the prescribed treatment.

Our view is that the selfish nature and the fears attached to it undermine the desire, courage, and strength we need to implement a therapist's good counsel. What we *naturally* encounter in our hearts are various degrees of selfishness, anger, envy, jealousy, laziness, self-defensiveness, pride, greed, and a plethora of other human characteristics that work like landmines in our relationships. No one has to teach us these traits.

Any parent has experienced the frustration of teaching a child about good behavior only to find that the instruction has been overshadowed by the child's selfish will. My wife and I (Glenn) have repeatedly taught our children about the importance of putting others first and sharing. But the next thing we see is our two kids bickering over who will get the first bowl of ice cream. Setting limits, disciplining, and teaching children are still essential roles for parents, but those alone are not enough. Most of the time, my kids *know* what's right and wrong, but the application of this knowledge is weakened by the selfish nature.

It is interesting to note a similarity between therapy's limitation and the insufficiency of the Old Testament Law. God provided humankind with divine wisdom about how to live. The Scriptures provide a perfect portrait of human nature: beings created in the image of God who have tragically turned away from his designs for our lives. The Old Testament story displays how humans, even with God's revealed wisdom in hand, end up falling short. Therefore, even knowledge of God's perfect Law will be insufficient to bring about the character change needed for whole relationships. Paul made this point as well, saying that the Law only makes us aware of all the ways we fail to meet its demands,[8] and "what the law was powerless to do in that it was *weakened by the sinful nature*, God did by sending his own Son."[9]

It is crucial to understand this central truth. If we depend only on human effort for character development, we will always fall short. Therapy, education, self-help methods—these can be a helpful part of character development, but these efforts alone are insufficient. Something deeper and more profound must occur in the human heart, something that addresses the selfish nature and gives us the inner resources that we lack.

Madelyn and Allan, even if they receive excellent therapy, will find themselves butting heads with their emotional weakness, selfish nature, and the limitations of their will. Where does that leave them?

They find themselves, surprisingly, sitting in the same boat with the illustrious apostle Paul.

BANKRUPT PEOPLE ARE RICH

You might remember that before Paul experienced his life-changing encounter with Jesus, he was a religious zealot bent on persecuting the fledgling groups of Christians. As a Pharisee, he lived on the basis of a superficial religiosity, a legalistic faith that never affected his inner being. Through the work of God, he came to see his true condition and his need for the forgiveness provided by Christ on the cross. He turned away from his former dependence on religious self-effort, realizing that his only hope was to embrace the grace of God through Jesus.

Then, in his letter to the Romans, Paul described his experience as a follower of Christ. Something radical had happened in his heart and mind. As a believer, he longed to live according to God's will. But though he set out to align his behavior with his godly desires, he often found it difficult to do what he knew was right. He would frequently do the wrong things that in his mind he didn't want to do. The problem, he said, was that another "law" opposed the godly desires of his mind. This law was his selfish nature, and it repeatedly upended his desire to do what was right and good.

What Paul described is the same limitation inherent to the therapeutic process. Paul portrayed the futility of attempting to change human behavior only on the basis of self-effort. At the end of his discussion, he threw up his hands and admitted, "What a wretched man I am! Who will rescue me from this body of death?" But he didn't end in despair. He found a hopeful solution. "Thanks be to God—through Jesus Christ our Lord!"[10]

If we are attentive to God as we pass through difficult situations, we can live from a foundation of hope, even when our circumstances are as harsh as Madelyn and Allan's. It's through difficult experiences that we begin to discover our inadequacies. But now these problems don't lead us to despair.

The realization of our limitations opens the door for God to work in our hearts. How we respond to these realities is crucial to the outcome of our lives.

Following the model of life Paul described, we need to appropriate and live on the basis of God's grace. In his grace we can admit our failures and limitations, and then *rely on God's strength*. This response leads us to authenticity, further growth, and the ability to live a full and abundant life.

In the next chapter, we will describe the ways God works in our lives to help us become Christlike and therefore to live out the four essentials of relational wholeness.

QUESTIONS FOR DISCUSSION

1. One of the purposes for the story of Madelyn and Allan is to show how each of the four essentials is interdependent with the others. It takes all four, working together, for a relationship to thrive. In chapter 7 we saw how integrity and love must work together. In the same way, the others must be there in the relationship for it to be whole. Consider the following:
   - Why does maintaining one's integrity require humility?
   - Why does it take humility to love another person?
   - What is the connection between forgiveness and integrity?
   - What is the connection between humility and forgiveness?
2. What would you do if you were Madelyn?
3. What do a therapist's counsel, the Old Testament Law (see Romans 3:19-20), and the apostle Paul (see Romans 7:14-24) have in common?
4. Where does that leave us?

Chapter 10

A DYNAMIC PARTNERSHIP WITH GOD

A poor, bedraggled, alcoholic woman missing several front teeth often came to my house (Glenn's) to beg for bus fare. My wife, Michelle, always attended her at the front gate. She doubted that the woman was using the money for bus fare, but nevertheless she always gave her something.

One day after Michelle had given the woman the full amount of the fare, she saw her at another house begging for more. The woman knew that Michelle had caught on to her scheme, so, probably due to her embarrassment, she didn't show up at our house again for months.

The next time she appeared, the woman looked more weary and worn than ever. Michelle met her at the front gate and the woman had the gall to ask for bus fare again. Michelle was peeved that the woman would lie yet another time, but she decided to go back in the house and get some money. Numerous critical thoughts ran through Michelle's mind as she pulled together the cash. She wondered how many other houses the woman had already visited.

As she walked back outside with the money and placed the money into the woman's dirty hand, Michelle suddenly realized how wrong it was for her to be so judgmental. Here was a woman who had nothing, an eternal being reduced to begging in order to survive. And yet Michelle, in her thoughts, had been critical and condescending.

After receiving the money, the woman said to her, "God bless you." Michelle knew right then that God had used the poor woman to teach her something. As the woman walked away, Michelle realized that she, like the woman at her door, was a broken beggar in desperate need of God's generosity. Michelle was reminded that we all come impoverished to God's door, completely lacking in righteousness and unable to heal ourselves.

At the end of the last chapter, we described how difficult it is to live out the four essentials on the basis of self-effort alone. As soon as we try to apply them, we confront the weaknesses of our selfish nature. As paradoxical as it might seem, we are blessed when we recognize this inner poverty.

One way God blesses us is to help us comprehend our destitute condition. We need this awareness, otherwise we will never be receptive to God's powerful work in our lives. As long as we believe in our self-sufficiency, we won't open our hearts to the true treasures he longs to give us.

For this reason, Jesus said: "Blessed (happy, fulfilled) are the poor in spirit." Then he says, "blessed are those who mourn," those who are "meek," and those who "hunger and thirst for righteousness."[1]

Author Wim Rietkerk expressed well the nature of God's blessings:

[A blessing] is not . . . . holy water sprinkled over something, or a thoughtless ritual before a meal. . . . The blessing has the function of a weeding machine, one could say. It cuts out all the weeds, and it confronts each of us and our whole nations with the fact that we are a garden full of weeds. . . . Asking for God's blessing is not just asking for victory or prosperity or peace of mind. It is asking for the weeding machine in our own lives, to fight the curse.[2]

The purpose of God's blessing, even on those occasions when it is painful, is for us to flourish. Imagine a field of dry winter grass. Then the spring rains come. All of a sudden, the field explodes with color and life. When Jesus talked about blessing, he had something like this in mind for our lives. Without him we are a dry field. But those who recognize their spiritual poverty, those who mourn over their poor condition, those who are meek, and those who hunger for what is holy and pure—these are the people who will flourish.

In the *Voyage of the Dawn Treader*, one of the classic children's books by C. S. Lewis, a lazy, complaining boy named Eustace lives according to his selfish nature, and as a result he finds himself lost and alone in a deep canyon. There Eustace discovers a dragon's lair full of treasure. After falling asleep on a pile of gold and gems, he wakes up to find that he has turned into a dragon. "He realized that he was a monster cut off from the whole human race. An appalling loneliness came over him," Lewis wrote.[3]

After several days, overwhelmed by the harsh reality of his condition, Eustace slides into depression. His friends try to console him, but they have no power to change him back into Eustace the boy.

One night, unable to sleep, he sees a huge lion coming toward him. It is Aslan (who represents Jesus in the stories by Lewis). The lion tells Eustace to follow him to the top of a mountain where there is a garden and a large pool of clear water. Eustace longs to enter the water, hoping it will ease his pain. But Aslan says he must first remove his dragon scales and skin. Eustace tries to scratch off the scales, but when he removes a layer, he finds more thick skin below. Tearing off layer after layer, he realizes that it is impossible. Then the lion says, "You will have to let me undress you." Eustace had discovered his spiritual poverty and the futility of self-reliance.

Eustace is afraid of Aslan's claws, but now, having acknowledged his own inability, he entrusts his destiny to the lion. Aslan makes some deep and painful cuts through the dragon skin, peeling it away until it is completely removed and piled in a heap. The operation hurt, but it is a blessing: Eustace is a boy again. Aslan then dresses him in new, clean clothing. Eustace has a new life. The whole experience makes him more humble and gentle. Most importantly, he has a sincere love for his friend Aslan, who saved his life.

Lewis concludes Eustace's story this way:

It would be nice, and fairly nearly true, to say that "from that time forth Eustace was a different boy." To be strictly accurate, he began to be a different boy. He had relapses. There were still many days when he could be very tiresome. But most of those I shall not notice. The cure had begun.[4]

As we have said, the four essentials are not a self-help method; they are character traits. Therefore, in order for us to experience whole relationships, our inner nature must be changed into the likeness of Jesus. This is obviously no small requirement. It is a life-long process born out of an ongoing, intimate walk with God.

My (Jim's) father is about to celebrate his one hundredth birthday. A few months ago, the two of us had an unforgettable conversation. We were reminiscing about our lives, the good times and the hardships and what it all means. And he said, "God is still working on me." It's remarkable that a man his age, who has spent nearly his entire life walking faithfully with God, could realize that God had more work to do in his life.

This is a good lesson for all of us. The believer's purpose in life is no longer the pursuit of self-actualization, but to "become mature, attaining to the whole measure of the fullness of Christ."[5] If we really understand the magnitude of "the fullness of Christ," it will be obvious that we could never in this life reach such a high standard. But we are called to persevere toward that destiny for as long as we are alive. As we live in this direction, we will experience real, substantial inner growth.

A FIRM FOUNDATION FOR LIFELONG GROWTH

As we discussed in chapter 4, those who believe in Christ and accept his forgiveness gain a new place in an unconditional relationship with God. This permanent and secure standing is the launch pad for a lifetime of character development.

Paul could barely contain his joy as he wrote a letter to his friends in Ephesus about our new identity as believers, declaring that God has "blessed us in the heavenly realms with every spiritual blessing in Christ."[6] God adopted us as his own children. He has showered us with his grace and love.

It's not that we're better than anyone else. Our new status is a gift, not something that we have earned. We have no basis for pride. "For it is by grace that you have been saved," Paul said, "through faith—and this not from yourselves, it is the gift of God—not by works, so that no one can boast."[7]

Imagine you have an adolescent daughter who comes home drunk after a party. She can barely walk in the door, and she can't complete a sentence. You are appalled and frightened. She is obviously not following the family rules. You've taught her never to get drunk, but not only did she drink too much, she also drove home plastered.

But notice that your daughter came home to *you*. She doesn't think about it, but there is no doubt in her mind that you are still her parent even though she comes home smelling like a brewery. She knows her behavior would never make her a nonchild.

Likewise, her terrible behavior never calls into question your identity as her parent. Even the fact that you feel embarrassed and hurt about your daughter's lack of discipline is proof of your oneness and mutual identity. You feel the pain because she is an extension of you. The identity you share as father (or mother) and daughter transcends the improper behavior.

This is what God, in Christ, experiences with us. He has adopted us as his children. We are part of his family. We did nothing to earn our position in this family. Our identity is now unified with his identity. We have his name. And that family identity persists independently of our successes or failures in life. We might not always live according to the family identity, but God will always be our father, and we'll always be his children.

These truths, which provide the basis for hope and meaning, give us inner strength to persevere. When we are guilty or feel accused, we know that we are still God's children. When the selfish nature trips us and we fall, we need not despair because God continues to love us as his own children. He will hold us strong in the absolute truth of his love.[8] And that assurance of ultimate security enables us to get back in the game and to press on even if we've messed up our lives.

Even when rejected by others, Jesus has established our firm standing and value. "If God is for us, who can be against us?" said Paul. "No, in all these things we are more than conquerors through him who loved us."[9] This truth does not remove the suffering we might encounter in our relationships, but it gives us an unshakeable foundation on which to stand in the middle of life's difficulties. In all things we are secure. Therefore, even if we fail, we always know how to get back home.

It is essential for each of us to understand and rely on this truth. God's grace establishes our relationship with him, and this permanent relationship is the foundation for the ongoing process of character development.

RATS IN THE CELLAR

Although full of great intentions, we soon find an obstacle to the outworking of our God-given identity. The selfish nature's rule over our hearts has resulted in habits, response patterns, and impulse reactions that undermine our relationships. Even though we are following Christ, the selfish nature is still active. The old habits linger in our lives. Anger, lying, criticism, or self-absorption can reside under the surface, often unobserved.

Josh watched his fifteen-year-old daughter, Amy, begin to withdraw from the family and move toward a troubling circle of friends that practiced a destructive lifestyle. Whenever he and his wife, Kim, would try to talk to her, Amy would become aggressive and sullen, shutting them both out. It was frightening.

One day, in the middle of a confrontation with Amy, Josh lost his temper and slapped her face hard. Josh immediately realized what he had done. The nemesis of his life, his anger, was back, and at a time when he could least afford it.

This wasn't the first time Josh's anger had gotten him into

trouble. It was there when he was a child, and he had carried it into his marriage. On several occasions over the years, Josh had frightened Kim with his angry reactions. This had already begun to undermine their mutual trust. A few months earlier, Josh, recognizing his need for help, had sought out a therapist. The therapist helped him understand the origins and causes of his anger. Life improved, as did Josh and Kim's marriage.

But now, in a nanosecond, the nightmare was back. The slap provoked Amy to even deeper resentment and rebellion. Angered and disgusted by his behavior, Kim reacted by protecting her daughter from Josh. He was devastated.

C. S. Lewis called these lurking habits "rats" that hide in the cellar of our lives. They usually show up as automatic reactions to spontaneous circumstances. "If there are rats in a cellar you are most likely to see them if you go in very suddenly," Lewis wrote. "But the suddenness does not create the rats; it only prevents them from hiding. In the same way, the suddenness of the provocation does not make me an ill-tempered man; it only shows me what an ill-tempered man I am. The rats are always in the cellar."[10] They are what the Bible describes as our sinful nature.[11]

Personality traits, such as perfectionism, also play a role. One's temperament can produce both positive and negative results. Personal strengths always have a flipside that can be hurtful if they are not carefully tempered. A man who is a perfectionist will usually be a valuable employee, but he could be overly demanding when it comes to his expectations of others. A person who is melancholic is usually sensitive and relational, but she may find it difficult to make decisions and to lead. Others struggle with impatience, compulsions, or the need to always be in control.

Ironically, we naturally, habitually nurture the rats that do so much damage to our relationships. For ten years Ben struggled with a drug addiction. All of his choices were centered on satisfying his selfish nature, the desires of his body, his longing for a chemical high. When he wasn't using drugs, he was overwhelmed by depression. He was in a deadly tailspin.

Ben knew some friends who read the Scriptures, and they invited him to participate. He sometimes showed up with blood-shot eyes and a nervous tic, but he learned a lot about the truth of God's love for him. It took a while for these ideas to settle into his mind and soul. But he began to understand what Christ had done for him on the cross, and he began to show remorse about his failures. Finally, Ben put his trust in God.

Already something had changed in Ben. Now, in his mind and heart, he longed to do what was right in God's eyes. He hated the drug-addict life with all its dark alleys and lies and fear. He wanted to live a different life, one with meaning and good relationships. There was just one problem: He could not overcome the physical addiction. The temptations were relentless. Driving by a certain street would remind him of where to buy drugs. Beer commercials would stimulate his desire for another high. A bad day at work would make him want to use drugs to relieve the stress. Even taking aspirin for a headache would fuel his desire for drugs and all the other physical pleasures attached to them.

His inability to control these impulses frustrated him. He had surrendered his heart to God and accepted God's love, but the addiction continued to drag him down. Then a friend showed him those verses in Romans that we discussed in the last chapter. Paul wasn't an addict, but Ben saw that Paul's life had similarities to his own life.

"So I find this law at work," Paul wrote about himself. "When I want to do good, evil is right there with me. For in my inner being I delight in God's Law; but I see another law at work in the members of my body, waging war against the law

173

of my mind and making me a prisoner of the law of sin at work within my members."[12]

These words resonated with Ben. He saw that Paul's "inner being," or heart, had surrendered to God and his deepest desire was to live according to God's law. Now Paul hated his old ways and had started traveling a different path. But the selfish nature still had a disturbing influence in his life. This was Ben's experience too.

Eventually, with God's help, Ben was able to overcome the downward pull of his addiction. But it was not easy or immediate. For more than a decade he had fed his body any and every pleasure it had desired. By living to please his selfish desires, he had gradually established a set of deeply ingrained and destructive habits, life patterns, and ways of responding. Now, as he experienced the horrific outcome of these habits, he found that they would not be easily broken.

Little by little, with strength and encouragement from God, he was able to make exceptions to his old response patterns. Some days were better than others, but as time passed, new behavior patterns formed. He was gradually able to choke off the oxygen flow to the old habits and live in new and healthy ways. Today, the old temptations still linger, but their influence is less powerful. There remains a long road to travel, but everyone can see the dramatic differences in his life.

Most of us will never go through the severe trials Ben endured, but like Paul and Ben, we all struggle with the selfish nature to one degree or another. Since childhood, everyone has been forming habits and response patterns that undermine relationships. As believers we will experience a daily battle with these negative tendencies.

Fortunately, we are not left alone in our struggle. In fact, because we have already given God direct access to our hearts, he now has a base camp from which to work in all areas of our lives. He is at our side, in our hearts, working with us, helping us to turn away from the selfish nature and to form new habits that result in life and beauty.

God is personal, and he will work individually with each of us according to our specific needs. But there are several common ways that God helps us overcome the rats in the cellar. The Scriptures clearly describe the tangible ways that God can help us as we open our hearts to his involvement.

HOW GOD WORKS

The first thing God will do is *show* us the rats. We don't like to admit it, but all of us are, in one way or another, a pain in the neck to others. The degree to which we resist that truth becomes the measure of how hard it is for people to relate to us. I prefer not to look at my failings, and I don't want you to look, but because of God's grace and forgiveness, there is no need to be afraid of what we might find in the cellar. The grace described above means that when God brings his light to bear on the outposts of the selfish nature, we can be sure that he wants to build us up. When God corrects us, there is no doubt that his correction and discipline are about love not condemnation.

Therefore, we have freedom to be transparent before God and others. Our attitude should be like King David, who prayed:

> Search me, O God, and know my heart;
>   test me and know my anxious thoughts.
> See if there is any offensive way in me,
>   and lead me in the way everlasting.[13]

Knowing the damage his habits could cause, David begged and pleaded with God to bring light into the dark corners of his life and to change him. We won't change unless we come to that same point of desperation.

God's Spirit does this work through two significant means: His Word and our life experiences.

GOD'S WORD

God has spoken. Because the Bible is God's commentary on life, we can get our bearings from it even in the most confusing times. It stands as a reality check against all the other voices, even though those voices might be more appealing to the selfish nature.

The Scriptures hold much wisdom and knowledge, but they also speak to us personally. Sometimes they affirm and encourage us at just the right moment. At other times, they open our eyes to our "offensive ways," as David put it. They are precise and personal. As the writer of Hebrews said, "For the word of God is living and active. Sharper than any double-edged sword, it penetrates even to dividing soul and spirit, joints and marrow; it judges the thoughts and attitudes of the heart."[14]

For people who read the Bible or hear it taught, the meaning of these words is clear. For example, we might find ourselves reading the account of the poor woman at the temple who gave away everything she had. It's a simple story. Then we read about how the religious leaders poured large sums of cash into the temple coffers as a means of obtaining applause from men. Even though they practiced generosity, they did it just to bolster their egos, to gain the praise of their peers. Then we see that Jesus was totally unimpressed by these guys. What got his attention was the pure heart of the poor woman who dropped just two cents into the bin.

As we read the story, God exposes something in our heart that we hadn't recognized. We realize that we have been doing good things, but that our motive has been to win eulogies from people, to be noticed and praised. It suddenly hits us that we're just like the Pharisees. God has shown us how prone we are to seeking our own glory. And then we realize how that tendency has been affecting our relationships, leading us to use people in order to bolster our self-image.

This healthy dynamic—between the Scriptures and our hearts—is an essential element of personal growth. The Scripture unearths all the stuff we'd rather keep buried in the backyard. But it does so as God's instrument of love, not condemnation. He is helping us grow.

LEARNING FROM EXPERIENCE

God fills our lives with his abundant love. But there are times when he allows us to go through hardship as a means of refining our lives. As the book of Hebrews says, "Endure hardship as discipline; God is treating you as sons. . . . No discipline seems pleasant at the time, but painful. Later on, however, it produces a harvest of righteousness and peace *for those who have been trained by it.*"[15]

Experience alone doesn't make us wise. A man decides to play golf, but he's had no training. He gets out on the golf course, and stroke after stroke, his ball ends up hooking and slicing out of bounds. His game is terrible. Now let's imagine that he never sought help from a golf instructor. He would continue to do everything wrong and spend his day looking for balls in the rough, never understanding what he had been doing wrong.

We have all gone through painful experiences without really understanding the causes of our suffering. God often allows us to go through difficult experiences in order to help us recognize our need for help. But the real growth happens only as God's Word enables us to understand what habits are causing us to bungle our relationships. As God's Word speaks to our experiences, we can, with God's involvement, begin to correct our bad habits. To be humble before God is to have a willingness to learn from our mistakes and to be eager for God to coach us.

Our friend Bill is a gifted medical doctor with a brilliant mind. Medical school came easily for him. His diagnostic ability soon put him among the elite within his profession. But his greatest aspiration was to have a good marriage and family. In his forties, he finally met someone he really loved. They married and had children. But then things began to fall apart.

Bill's primary medical asset—his diagnostic skill—became a prevailing factor in the marriage's collapse. In arguments with his wife, he would use truth like a scalpel—objective, precise, but devastating. Rather than listening, he would diagnose and do verbal surgery. This left her in pieces.

At first, as Bill's divorce proceeded, he blamed his wife. After all, she had left him. If she had been willing to persevere they could have made it through the crisis, he reasoned. Casting blame is as far as many couples ever get, but a friend helped him see that his use of truth had not been mixed with love. He realized that, in fact, he had caused the relational crisis.

Bill was honest enough to see his failures in the marriage. Instead of hiding from God to protect his pride, he became humble and transparent. He was willing to be trained by the experience. And as a result there has been significant character development in this area of Bill's life. Now he's come to realize the interdependency of truth and love. He's made great strides, becoming a person who tempers his opinions and observations with a spirit of love.

THE INNER WORK OF THE HOLY SPIRIT

Up to now we've seen that God provides us with amazing resources as he works to mold our character into the likeness of Jesus. He has helped dethrone the selfish nature from our hearts and instilled in us a new desire for living according to his relational design for life. He has provided his grace, which gives us complete security in our relationship with him. In a spirit of fatherly love, he reveals the specific trouble spots of our character through his Word and our experiences. The Spirit of God is involved in all of this.

Jesus promised that the Spirit would lead us into all truth. He called the Spirit "the Counselor," someone who would give us truthful guidance and wisdom in relation to our personal situations.[16] This guidance will always be consistent with the Scriptures and the character of Jesus.

The New Testament describes his work as being similar to a communication link between the heart of God and our hearts. He is the person in the Trinity who makes heart-level, day-to-day intimacy between us and God possible.

During my (Glenn's) first months of life in Brazil, my wife and I witnessed a brutal murder. As it was happening, I longed to pull my family to safety. The memory of a friend's house in the mountains of Colorado came to mind, a place of peace and security. I wanted to be there, to take my family to a safe place. Then, the next morning, I read the following verse from the book of Psalms:

In the LORD I take refuge.
How then can you say to me:
"Flee like a bird to your mountain."[17]

That settled it for me. True safety is only found in God. His Spirit had counseled me.

I (David) went through about seven years of serious doubts about God. I had experienced some difficult situations in a church. I was studying psychology in a graduate program. God seemed to be removed, and I had a lot of spiritual inertia. Then, one night as I sat on my back patio, I suddenly felt the presence of God. I felt filled and touched by him in a personal way. He came and found me. It was the most transcending night of my life.

Paul wrote, "The Spirit searches all things, even the deep things of God. For who among men knows the thoughts of a man except the man's spirit within him? In the same way no one knows the thoughts of God except the Spirit of God."[18]

But the Spirit's work does not stop there. He takes the deep thoughts of God and reveals them to our hearts. Again Paul said,

> "No eye has seen,
>   no ear has heard,
> no mind has conceived
>   what God has prepared for those who love
>   him" —

but God has revealed it to us by his Spirit.[19]

All of this profound work by the Spirit happens quietly in our hearts. He does not force his will upon us, but he does powerfully influence our heart and mind. The actual work of the Spirit is, therefore, not visible. But the effect of his work will be very apparent in a person's attitudes and behaviors.

In one of the most important passages about the Holy Spirit, Paul said that the work of the Spirit was obvious in the lives of his friends in Corinth, that the changes in their lives could never have been the result of mere human effort: "You show that you are a letter from Christ, the result of our ministry, written not with ink but *with the Spirit of the living God, not on tablets of stone but on tablets of human hearts.*"[20]

What Paul describes here is the profound work of God in the depths of the human soul. This is the only way that growth toward a Christlike character can happen. Self-help methods, therapy, parenting, education — all of this can be used by God to change our character, but without this penetrating and powerful work of the Spirit in our hearts, all of those efforts will fall short. Only the Spirit can touch the depths of our hearts.

We can count on the Spirit's influence in our inner being, but he leaves it to us to decide how we will respond. If we respond in humility to his revelations about our character, he will begin to change us in ways that would be humanly impossible. We usually don't *feel* any different. It is change that happens over time. But the more we walk with God in humility, the more we take our failures to him in confession and prayer, the more we will see him change the bad habits of our lives.

This approach to life, which is *based on humility*, is dramatically different from self-help methods, which rely exclusively on human capacity. This is one of the principles that most distinguishes the Christian faith from our self-help culture.

I (Jim) struggled for years with impatience. It took a long time for me to even realize that I was impatient. I used to think that everyone else was just slow. This rat in my cellar complicated many of my interactions with family and colleagues. As God revealed my problem, I began to consistently pray about it and confess it to God. I admitted my inability to change by my own efforts alone. I asked God to help me.

Then, a number of years later, my colleagues at work and I took some time to evaluate one another. Everyone, about twelve of us, wrote down two strengths and one weakness about each person on the team. Then each person received the observations of the others.

After the exercise was over, one of my closest friends asked me how others had evaluated my strengths and weaknesses. I told my friend that the observations I had received couldn't have been accurate because so many people had described me as a patient person, when, in fact, I struggled daily with impatience. But my friend, who knew me very well, said that he was one of the people who wrote that I was patient. Then he proceeded to describe what he saw in me that led him to make that observation. His comment both surprised and pleased me. Only then did I realize that God had, over time, brought about change in my life. Even though I hadn't perceived it, other people in my relational circle noticed the difference.

To follow Jesus is to live a fascinating paradox. We find that when we are strong, it is not because *we* are strong but because we are aware of our weaknesses and then lean on God's strength. As God explained it to Paul, "My grace is sufficient for you, for my power is made perfect in weakness." And Paul concluded, "I will boast all the more gladly about my weaknesses, so that Christ's power may rest on me."[21]

OUR RESPONSIBILITIES

A friend once invited me (Glenn) to climb a tall desert tower called Independence Monument. I had no climbing experience, so I was hesitant to accept the offer. But my friends were experts, and I knew I could trust them. Before long I was putting on climbing shoes and learning to use a carabiner.

After several hours of climbing, we arrived at the last and most difficult section of the route. An overhang jutted out between us and the pinnacle. My hand and forearm strength had burned out, and I lacked experience, so naturally I worried about my ability to surmount this most difficult section. But there was no way to turn back.

My friend shot up the steep face and bolted past the overhang without any difficulty. Then he called down and told me to start climbing. I went up another twenty feet and rested just below the overhang. After a deep breath, I confronted the overhang's underside by stretching up and backward. This shifted weight away from my legs and forced me to use even more arm and finger strength to hold myself on the rock. It didn't take long to realize that I was going to fall. So I yelled to my friend, begging him to hold the rope firm. Then I fell.

In a flash I was swinging back and forth like a clock pendulum, 350 feet in the air, heart pounding and adrenaline pumping. My friend had a grand time laughing at me—in a friendly way. (I think he was actually expecting and hoping that I would come off the rock.) I dangled for a while and pretended not to be afraid.

After a rest, I had to get back on the rock and start climbing again. I was able to start swinging and reattach myself to the rock. But I still needed to surpass the overhang. And, once again, I could not find the strength. So this time, my friend pulled the rope while I climbed. For real climbers this is cheating. For rookies it's essential. It wasn't pretty, but with his help I was able to get over the lip of the overhang and finish the climb.

Walking with God is a lot like that climb. We have limits, and we lack experience. There are times when progress is good, and there are days when it seems like we are getting nowhere. We struggle with fear and weariness. Sometimes we don't even feel like being nice, let alone being people who love and forgive. God will help us, but we have to do our part, get back on the rock, and climb.

The word *responsibility* means "able to respond." God made humans as beings who are able to respond to his initiatives and influence. While our self-effort alone is insufficient for bringing about the inner change that we need for whole relationships, it is essential that we do our part.

One of our primary responsibilities in relation to the process of character development is to care for our minds. Through the mind we form our way of seeing the world, our value system, and our perspectives. Therefore, the mind plays a crucial role in our decisions and behavior. For this reason, Paul said, "Do not conform any longer to the pattern of this world, but be transformed by the renewing of your mind."[22]

The natural inclination of humankind, however, is to make the selfish nature priority and truth secondary. And as long as the selfish nature controls the heart, the mind will reject any truth that conflicts with those self-centered desires.

One of the best examples of how this happens is a confession by British writer Aldous Huxley in his book *Ends and Means*. He was an atheist. In the following quote, Huxley said that he adopted atheism for no other reason than it gave him license to pursue his selfish desires:

> We don't know because we don't want to know. It is our will that decides how and upon what subjects we shall use our intelligence. . . . For myself as, no doubt, for most of my contemporaries, the philosophy of meaninglessness was essentially an instrument of liberation. The liberation we desired was simultaneously liberation from a certain political and economic system and liberation from a certain system of morality. We objected to the morality because it interfered with our sexual freedom.[23]

We are all prone to adopt false ideas in order to justify our self-centered desires. What Huxley chose on a philosophical level can quickly happen to us in our everyday decisions, attitudes, and behavior. It is easy to rationalize away our responsibility to serve, forgive, and live with integrity.

Thus, it is essential that we conform our thoughts and perspectives to God's truth even when it opposes our selfish nature. The closer we align our thoughts and beliefs to the reality God has established, the more harmonious and beautiful our lives will be.

In the context of our relationships, our mental framework should comprise the four essentials—integrity, love, humility, and forgiveness. These four character traits need to be at the forefront of our minds. As we consider our responsibilities at work and home, we can make integrity, love, humility, and forgiveness the template for our daily decisions. We can test ourselves using the four essentials as the standard.

- Am I doing what is right and true in my business practices?
- Am I actively serving and loving my wife (or husband) and children?
- Am I humble, taking the time to listen and understand people?
- Am I judging someone rather than forgiving him or her?

With this mental framework established, these thoughts must translate into action. But change doesn't happen with fireworks and drama. Transformation begins in the incidentals of one's life, in quiet, deep ways. Each day provides opportunities to practice the four essentials. Consider these potential scenarios:

INTEGRITY

A man who has struggled with telling lies his entire life finds himself caught between conflicting opportunities. He has scheduled a lunch meeting, but then his son invites him to spend the afternoon fishing. The time with his son is important, but to cancel a business meeting for a fishing trip might make him look bad among his business colleagues. So the man invents a small lie; he won't be able to keep the appointment because the office needs him to solve a sudden problem. He picks up the phone, but then he remembers the importance of truth. Rather than telling the lie, he makes the call, but honestly explains the situation and asks the person if it would be possible to reschedule.

This is not an insignificant step for this man. He's facing the reality of his history of lying. It seems incidental, but it is a major change of direction. He's no longer on autopilot, reacting without thinking. He has just made an exception to a lifetime habit of fudging his way through awkward situations. He experiences the freedom of having only one story going on in life, the true story. As Jesus said, "The truth will set you free."[24]

LOVE

Another man comes home from work to find his wife frustrated and stressed after a really bad day. She angrily complains that he forgot to take out the trash before work and that now the garbage is going to stink in the garage for another week. His immediate response is anger and defensiveness, but then he remembers the nature of love, that it is serving—building up the other. So he prepares something to drink and invites her to join him on the deck. He listens to her, and they talk about the day. As a result, he brings healing to his wife, and he takes another step toward a new behavior pattern.

HUMILITY

A woman is in conflict with a coworker who has been competing with her for a better position in the company. After months of cold interaction, she realizes that she has a problem with pride and remembers the importance of humility in her relationships. So she chooses to set her pride aside and mentally declares an armistice. She gives her own professional future into God's hands. Her attitude toward her coworker begins to change from stonewalling to inclusion. This attitude change becomes apparent in their daily encounters, and it defuses the conflict without her saying a word. It's a struggle, but her heart is free.

FORGIVENESS

Then there's an irresponsible sixteen-year-old who is causing his parents grief. He'll never get into college if he doesn't improve his grades, but he has an aversion to anything that looks like work. The auto insurance costs have tripled because of his accidents, but he doesn't seem to care. Communication between the son and his parents has all but disappeared. Understandably, the parents are filled with frustration, which leads them to critical attitudes. They realize that they have constructed a divisive wall of judgments against him and recognize that they have alienated their son in their hearts. They ask God to help them release their grudges, and then they begin to take initiatives to change the relationship.

Each of these little steps seems, in itself, to be almost incidental, but each of them is a step of progress toward profound character change.

There is one more important element to the Christian adventure. To grow in the four essentials requires us to be connected to a small circle of people. We can't become Christlike if we're living in isolation. We need one another. That is the subject of the next chapter.

QUESTIONS FOR DISCUSSION

1. This chapter explores the actual process of change, the dynamics that need to be operative if character transfor-

mation is to occur. The chapter begins with a discussion on the change that occurs in one's identity upon submission to Christ. The person becomes a *child of God*, a *member of His family*. What does that have to do with personal transformation?

2. In what ways are the Scriptures necessary to the process?
3. What part does the Holy Spirit play? How can you tell if the Holy Spirit is working in you?
4. Suppose you struggle with lust, anger, an addiction, or whatever. You have become aware of the destructive power of that pattern, and you decide you must become freed of it. What will need to happen in order for you to gain that freedom?

Chapter 11

CLOSE COMPANY

P aul Tournier, a Swiss psychiatrist and Christian author, became an orphan by the time he was six-years old. His father died first. Then, some years later, his mother was also gone from his life. He and his sister were raised by a loving aunt and uncle, but the death of his mother caused him to fall into what he called a "black hole." Believing that he could no longer count on anyone, he became introspective, solitary, timid, and unable to develop friendships.

Although the early school years for Tournier were what he called an impersonal experience, there was one man who noticed him and sought to help. He was Tournier's Greek teacher. Over time a strong friendship developed. According to Tournier, the teacher "initiated a dialogue that pulled me out of my isolation." The friendship lasted for years, even after Tournier was no longer his student.

This important relationship enabled Tournier to break free from his timidity and make progress in his education and profession. He went on to become a doctor, but there were still significant wounds hidden under the surface. Through college and residency, he continued to use academics and constant activity as a means of hiding the inner struggles related to the deaths of his parents. He was still "a recluse at heart."

When he was thirty-four-years old, Tournier met another person whose personal attention launched him to new levels of growth. He was a Dutchman and a high-level financial analyst at the League of Nations. What captured Tournier was his friend's willingness to openly share his personal struggles and failures. Because of his friend's transparency, Tournier said he could no longer just talk about his activities and ideas. He had to expose his own soul too. So, in one conversation, he finally unveiled the pain related to his parents' deaths.

"It was the first time I had ever put into words what I had suffered in being an orphan, and I was in tears as I did so," he wrote.[1]

From that point on, Tournier was a changed man. The experience of deep, transparent, personal connection overwhelmed him with joy and healing. He began to seek increased transparency with the people in his relational network. And he changed the spirit of his work. He decided to dedicate his life to making the medical profession more personal and human. He wrote numerous books to help people find meaning in an impersonal society. These have helped thousands of people grow closer to one another and to God.

Tournier's two friends probably had no idea what a strong impact they would have on his life. And they could not have comprehended how their hidden investments would end up benefiting so many people through Tournier's books and career. But it was through these friendships, Tournier said, that he "was discovering the personal mode of relationship, and finding out how fruitful it is for oneself and for the other person, and how it helps to bind us together, so that we open our hearts to each other on what we have lived and felt."[2]

This type of personal and loving attention is what the New Testament writers most valued. If we look carefully at the Scriptures—past the ideas, doctrine, and theology—we see that the Christian life is above all a relational life. For this reason we find a phrase that appears repeatedly in the letters that the apostles wrote to the first century followers of Jesus. They said things such as, "be devoted to one another . . . honor one another. . . . Rejoice with those who rejoice; mourn with those who mourn. Live in harmony with one another";[3] "encourage one another and build each other up;"[4] "Do not use your freedom to indulge the sinful nature; rather, serve one another in love."[5]

The whole purpose of God has been to restore his relationship with mankind. He tears down the dividing walls by his Son's death on the cross. And then he sets out to form a family of people, searching for any who will accept his offer. Building this family is his highest priority. Naturally, he longs for those who follow him to form strong bonds with one another.

Step back and look at God's relational heart, the death and resurrection of his Son, and the four essential character traits modeled by Jesus: Where does it all lead us? The answer is as simple as it is profound. It all points to a life focused on one another.

THE PERSONAL FOCUS OF JESUS

One of the most surprising characteristics of Jesus' life was how little he had to show at the end of it. He left no major church. Most of the people at the time rejected him. Only a handful of people came to his funeral. One of his closest friends, Judas, betrayed him, and another, Peter, denied him three times. By all worldly standards, he could have been considered a total failure.

The apparent lack of tangible results in his life is even more ironic when we consider who he claimed to be and the grandiosity of his self-proclaimed mission. He said he came to save mankind and he went around talking about an eternal kingdom. He had a magnificent and broad vision. But all that he left behind was a rag-tag little group of people. When we compare the lofty claims of Jesus to the seemingly insignificant results of his life and work, what should we conclude?

As we look closely at this enigma, we find an important lesson for our lives, a principle that shreds our worldly definitions of success. Any serious consideration of his life forces us to reconsider the priorities we have established for our own lives. His life compels us to reevaluate the structure and routines of our existence. The principle we find in the life of Jesus is that God is accomplishing his plans when we focus on, care for, and invest in individuals in personal ways.

Look at the way Jesus operated. His primary impetus was to influence individuals on a personal level, according to their individual needs. He focused on a small circle of intimate relationships.

There are, of course, scenes of Jesus among the crowds. Throngs of people chased after him for a while. His fan club grew because of the miracles he performed. Most of us, if we were in his situation, would be ecstatic about the growing popularity and "effectiveness" of our work. What a great following! What success! But Jesus responded in a totally different way. According to John, Jesus knew that the people merely wanted him to be their political king, so he "withdrew again to a mountain by himself."[6] He knew that the crowds were not interested in a personal relationship with God.

Not surprisingly, most of the people in those crowds didn't stick with Jesus for long. It's clear that very few surrendered their hearts to his lordship.[7] He was "the narrow gate." But when everyone else abandoned him, his close friends and a handful of relatives remained. These were the people to whom Jesus had given personal attention.

Notice how the four Gospels give prominence to the personal exchanges he had with individuals — the adulterous woman, Nicodemus during that evening conversation, his personal care of the sick and lame, a centurion, his heartfelt encounters with Peter, a tax collector, and a prostitute. As the crowds gathered, Jesus zeroed in on individuals to address their spiritual and physical needs in a personal way. He sought opportunities to draw out the souls of people in one-on-one dialogues. In these discussions, he cut through the superficial and touched the true person.

The Gospels reveal Jesus as a man with intimate relationships, not a man establishing a public relations campaign. One of the best examples is found in the account of the death of Lazarus, the brother of Mary and Martha. It appears from John's writings that Jesus came to know Lazarus through his friendship with Mary, a woman known for having lived a sinful life. She was the same woman who, with a broken spirit, had poured expensive perfume on Jesus.[8] However he came to befriend Lazarus, the Scriptures say that Jesus had a close friendship with him and his sisters. Upon arriving at the grave, before he raised Lazarus from the tomb, Jesus wept. Everyone there noticed how much he cared for Lazarus.[9]

His personal friendships, which by the world's standards of success might have seemed so insignificant, ended up being the foundation for a movement that would change the world. Jesus was obviously focused on and committed to this overall mission in life. But his mission was never impersonal. The primary outworking of his goal was to make personal investments in individual lives.

In light of the high value Jesus gave to his small circle of relationships, what should we conclude? After his death and resurrection, the people who stayed with him to the end had to answer the same question. And the New Testament gives us a portrait of how they did so.

Even though they often fumbled and floundered, they carried the ball forward with perseverance and courage. But what is most compelling is the way they focused on developing love-filled, service-oriented relationships within small networks of family and friends, just as Jesus had modeled for them. It wasn't perfect, but they fostered tightly knit communities that were strikingly alive and personal in the middle of a harsh, impersonal Roman culture.

LESSONS FROM THE FIRST-CENTURY CHURCH

Today, the first thing that comes to mind when we think of church is a building, a place where we congregate at set times in the week. This familiar form defines church for both churchgoers and non-churchgoers alike. It's hard for us to imagine anything else. But the first-century church was so different that we would scarcely recognize what they did as being church at all.

There were no church buildings. One reason for that was because the early believers were often persecuted. At times they had to operate as an underground movement. But that wasn't the only reason they didn't think of church in terms of bricks and mortar.

The early believers understood the church to be people having a common bond in Jesus Christ and relating to one another as a family. In their minds, the church was not a place, or an organization or even a set of activities. To suggest "going to church" to a first-century follower of Christ would draw a blank look. "*Go* to church? *Do* church? What do you mean? We are church," they would respond. In fact, for them the Greek word we translate as "church" —*ekklesia* — was nothing more than a commonly used word to describe a get-together. For them, meeting a few friends for a cup of coffee would have been an ekklesia.

These early Christians lived short, hard lives, but they probably had one advantage in comparison to our present-day circumstances. For them, work, family, and faith were more integrated than for us. In the Greco-Roman culture, the household (*oikos*) was the basic social unit. It was also the basic economic unit. It encompassed the extended family, a trade and work, education, leisure, and religion. Women made an economic contribution to the family without having to be separated from the children. Fathers worked alongside the children, teaching them the family trade and the important lessons of life. Servants, tutors, and artisans were included as household members. The head of the household led the family, managed its business, and defended its traditions. A household was self-sustaining, like a small ecosystem. Our word *economy* has its origins in this structure, coming from the root *oiko-nomia.*

By contrast, these aspects of our lives today tend to be compartmentalized. Our kids go to school in different places while mom and dad go to separate offices. In the afternoons, the kids go to extracurricular activities. Mothers feel the tension between work and providing a healthy home for the children. Fathers struggle to find time to influence their kids. We might manage to eat dinner together and watch a little TV before bed.

Upon accepting Jesus, the first-century believers didn't invent any new religious forms. Rather, they integrated their new faith into the existing structure of their lives—the oikos. They gave up idol worship, of course, but they wore the same clothing, kept the same weekly schedule, and maintained the same vocations. And most, if not all of the interaction, continued to happen in homes.

The very first believers were Jews in Jerusalem. Meeting in the temple was part of their cultural routine. So they used it as a gathering place. But even these people gave emphasis to an intimate setting and a small network of friends. As the record says, "Every day they continued to meet together in the temple courts. They broke bread in their homes [*oikov*] and ate together with glad and sincere hearts."[10]

As the news of Jesus' resurrection spread to other cities and regions, the new believers in these areas had few or no cultural ties with the Jewish traditions. These ethnically diverse people didn't have access to a temple. They wanted to abandon the various forms of paganism that were prominent at the time and follow Christ. So they just lived their new faith within their already existing relational networks, from household to household.

There is every indication from the New Testament record that this form was deliberate, not just circumstantial. Paul and his team made a conscious effort to build and maintain a personal, closely knit, small, and highly relational expression of the church. One city might have numerous Christian households. On some occasions, depending on the city, there is evidence that several households would gather together. When the early believers met, they always gathered in someone's home. The number of people involved was very small.

Robert Banks, in his book *Paul's Idea of Community*, emphasizes that Paul and others did everything possible to sustain highly personal, relational, and small networks of believers. Banks says that Paul "sought to build up enduring relationships of an organic, or only loosely organized, rather than institutional, character."[11]

These small networks of relationships were not insulated from the rest of society. The early believers were by no means cloistered people. Sometimes they experienced persecutions and civic exclusion but not because they had adopted a foreign way of living. Overall they were ingrained in the normal, everyday culture and economy. What changed were their attitudes, character, and values.

There are many good examples of these intimate relational networks. Soon after the apostles Paul and Silas arrived in the city of Philippi, they met a businesswoman named Lydia. Paul said, "When she and the members of her *household* were baptized, she invited us to her home [oikos]. 'If you consider me a believer in the Lord,' she said, 'come and stay at my house [oikos].' And she persuaded us."[12]

But then Paul and Silas ended up in a Philippian jail. An earthquake at midnight shattered the prison, and all the prisoners were set loose. The jailer, knowing he would be killed for allowing the prisoners to escape, took out his sword and was about to kill himself when Paul stopped him. He assured the man that the prisoners hadn't escaped.

Scared to death, the jailer asked,

"Sirs, what must I do to be saved?"
They replied, "Believe in the Lord Jesus, and you will be saved—you and your *household*." Then they spoke the word of the Lord to him and to all the others in his *house*. . . . The jailer brought them into his *house* and set a meal before them; he was filled with joy because he had come to believe in God—he and his whole family."[13]

As far as we know, the church in the city of Philippi got its start with these two households. That was the pattern in all the other regions too. Over time, the church in a city would become a network of believing households, coordinated by a handful of mature people who had proven their integrity by caring well for their own households. In fact, a person's integrity and faithfulness at home was the primary criterion for someone who would care for the other households in a city.[14] Paul, in his farewell to the leaders of this network in the city of Ephesus, summarized his ministry there by saying, "You know that I have not hesitated to preach anything that would be helpful to you but have taught you publicly and from *house* to *house* [*oikous*]."[15]

THE FOUR ESSENTIAL CHARACTER TRAITS AND THE OIKOS

This model, the *oikos*, provides the perfect framework for character growth in relation to the four essentials. An intimate network of friends and family is indispensable for there to be any chance of personal growth in relation to integrity, love, humility, and forgiveness. A tightly knit setting provides a context for *living* the four essentials. We need one another for our own personal growth.

It's easy to be a fake in an Internet chat room. But when we are rooted in a small set of relationships, people know our deepest needs, understand our reactions, hear our words, and see our decisions. A group of people who know us intimately serves as a mirror that enables us to see who we are becoming.

Imagine what it must have been like for a first-century family to embrace the kingdom of God. Imagine yourself as the head of such a household. You're a metalworker. You, your wife, and your six children spend most days forging tools, mainly for farming. The oldest son runs the foundry and a son-in-law does the woodworking. The other children fit in wherever they're most needed.

Over time, you begin to see some interesting changes in a neighboring household. You learn that they have become followers of the Way, which was how the early believers defined themselves. There is something whole and real about them. Unlike most other men in the culture, the husband serves his wife and doesn't just treat her like a piece of property. The family is generous, opening their house to people in need. After some conversations with your neighbors about the facts of Jesus' life, you become convinced about Jesus and make a conscious decision to submit to him and follow him in the way he lived. Nobody is quite sure what this will imply, but today the orders for ploughs and rakes still need to be filled. So everyone goes back to work.

A long-time customer, who works for a wealthy landowner, enters your workshop and asks you to make eight axe heads and then bill the landowner for ten. The customer offers to split the extra money with you, arguing that the landowner has so much money that he will never know the difference.

You've done this deal before. In fact, this is what everyone in town does. If you don't, someone else will. But then you notice that your twelve-year-old son is watching. There's a question in his eyes. He is wondering how citizens of God's kingdom do business. And he is deciding what kind of person he will become. It's an awkward moment as you remember what one of your believing friends said: "Live a life worthy of the Lord."[16]

Stammering, you explain why you can't make the sale on dishonest terms. The customer leaves, angry, and promises never to do business with you again. You remember all the people you need to feed in your household, but something inside you feels peaceful and good.

In relation to love, the first century oikos also proved to be invaluable as people went through the harsh realities of life. People bonded together to help one another when there was economic crisis or sickness. "Christian values of love and charity had, from the beginning, been translated into norms of social service and community solidarity," wrote historian Rodney Stark about the early believers. "When disasters struck, the Christians were better able to cope, and this resulted in substantially higher rates of survival."[17]

Stark documents how diseases would ravage entire regions. Fear spread like wildfire. The Christians, because of the radical differences in their worldview, found comfort and hope, knowing that death was not the end of the story. They held firmly to a central teaching: Love one another as yourself. They might not have had much more theology than that, but it made a dramatic difference in the way they dealt with the pestilences that whipped through the regions of the time.

Stark said that many ancient extrabiblical documents give "tribute to the heroic nursing efforts of local Christians, many of whom lost their lives while caring for others." They comforted the dying and gave them proper burials. This was in contrast to the way most people at the time responded. The majority would send the sick away, throw them alive into the roads to die like animals, and, because of fear of contracting the disease, leave the corpses unburied.[18]

Over time, the believers' bold demonstrations of the "love one another" command enabled more Christians to survive the epidemics than nonbelievers. The higher survival rate also "produced a much larger proportion of Christians who were *immune*, and who could, therefore, pass among the afflicted with seeming invulnerability," said Stark.[19] Many people became followers of Christ because they were attracted by the sacrificial love among the Christians and because the Christians did so much to serve and care for their unbelieving neighbors.

Their love for one another was also evident in the routines of daily life. Robert Banks says that it was the small, intimate groups that made the "art of love" possible among the early believers:

> It is in the Spirit of Christ, then, that the early Christian communities sought to become communities of love, to become familial and familiar settings in which the art of love could be learned, to become places where the love that bound together Son and Father could be a visible, corporate reality in the lives of those who had committed themselves to the gospel.[20]

The early believers also managed to build a safe relational environment that allowed for emotional healing and character growth. This is a remarkable truth about the first-century believers. They dealt with relational struggles that included divorce, sexual immorality, and other conflicts. But all of these difficulties came out into the light. The groups were small, so everyone knew what was happening. People dealt with problems in truth, honesty, and confession. The reason this could happen is because they understood God's forgiveness and grace as provided by Jesus and his death.

The apostle John wrote that the Christian life demands that we "walk in the light."[21] Everyone is sinful, he said, but we are called to be open and confessional with God and with one another about our failures. The purpose of this transparency is to maintain "fellowship with one another."[22] John knew that sin could only be a barrier to intimacy if it remained hidden under layers of pride and fear. Once it was out in the open, people would experience the power of the "blood of Jesus, his Son," who "purifies us from all sin."[23] The key, in John's mind, was to prevent the struggle with sin from ruining the intimacy. We need the intimacy to win the struggle with sin! Our transparency and God's forgiveness result in relational growth and inner change.

As such, the small, home-based setting was purposefully valued as a natural means of helping the believers influence the culture and "the most conducive atmosphere in which they could give expression to the bond they had in common," said Banks.[24]

The early believers—meeting in homes, maintaining a form that fostered close relationships, and staying ingrained in the culture—realized they would need one another in order to grow in Christ. Paul repeatedly told his friends that they were part of a body, and that one part belonged to the other. He urged them to live intimate and interdependent lives. And that is what they did, at least for a while.

As the faith spread across the Roman Empire through the first three centuries after Christ, it eventually became the official religion of the state. As historian Paul Johnson writes,

> By the end of the fourth century, in fact, the Church had not only become the predominant religion in the Roman empire, with a tendency to be regarded as the official one, indeed as the only one. It had also acquired many of the external characteristics appropriate to its new status: official rank and privilege, integration with the social and economic hierarchy, splendid and elaborate ceremonial designed to attract the masses and emphasize the separateness of the priestly caste.[25]

The upside of this change was that it helped diminish persecutions against Christians. But there was also a downside. Constantine, emperor between AD 306 and 337, shifted state funding away from the pagan temples and gave it to Christians. As a result, "a faith that had been meeting in humble structures was suddenly housed in magnificent public buildings." And the clergy, formerly supported by local followers, now became recipients of state funding, thus giving them increased status and power.[26]

From this point forward, the church became increasingly hierarchical and less of a grassroots movement that spread relationally. Many people adopted Christianity as an external, add-on religious form, rather than as a matter of true conversion. Many parts of northern and western Europe became "superficially Christianized," unlike the early believers who had deep convictions and death-defying dedication to Jesus and their circle of relationships. Christian *religiosity* began to spread without much heart-level spiritual transformation.

In short, the personal expressions of the church continued, but only in the shadow cast by the state church. As such, Stark said that Constantine "destroyed its [the early Christian movement's] most attractive and dynamic aspects, turning a high-intensity, grassroots movement into an arrogant institution controlled by an elite who often managed to be both brutal and lax."[27]

Even though Constantine dramatically institutionalized the natural, organic, and relational dynamics of the faith, there were many efforts to reclaim the church's original characteristics. Stark said that the famous Protestant Reformation in the 1500s was preceded by many, many earlier but less famous reformations.[28]

We can't return to the first century, and we wouldn't want to if we could. Those were not the good old days. Life was hard and brutish. But we can take lessons from those early followers of Christ who lived out their faith in their households and shops. The same relational dynamic can be at work today. We must protect and sustain the relational and personal nature of the Christian faith. One way or another, intimate relationships need to be the primary expression of Christian life.

Our need for intimate, mutual support remains unabated. We need it to grow in character and to persevere over our lifetimes in that growth. Support of this kind makes the difference between a train wreck in one's life and a successful journey. In our impersonal world, what people most need, as much now as in the first century, is love and personal care.

RECOVERING THE OIKOS

The point here is not to argue for one form of Christianity versus another, but rather to establish personal, intimate, transparent relationships as our principle focus in life. Whatever form our lives take, it should serve this foundational pursuit.

We need a countermovement against our self-oriented and materialistic times. What would it look like to really refocus our priorities on the people in our lives? What would it require of us? What would we have to sacrifice? What would be the benefits?

It would be foolish to try to recreate the exact form of the first century oikos, but we are still called to implement the timeless "one another" way of life described so frequently in the New Testament. We need to carefully consider whether our lives are centered on the essence of Christian life—to "be devoted to one another in brotherly love."[29]

In 1963, my wife, Marge, and I (Jim) moved to Brazil. A year later we were joined by another couple, Ken and Carol Lottis. Our vision was to lay foundations for a movement among students and professionals who, because of faith in Christ, would bring more relational wholeness to the Brazilian society.

The culture at the time was politically charged. Students were often Marxist, anti-government, anti-religion, and anti-American. Most of them did not believe the Bible, but they saw in us an opportunity to explore their existential questions with no strings attached, without having to join anything or become religious. Before long there was a steady stream of students hanging out in our house to look at the life and identity of Jesus.

Ken and I watched the growing numbers and began to worry. What are we going to do with all these people? Start a church? If we formed a congregation, we feared the message of Christ would lose mobility in the culture. And we wanted them to live out the essential principles of the New Testament in ways that were natural to them as Brazilians.

As we struggled with this dilemma, both Ken and I were devoting hours every day to mentoring students who were taking their first look at Jesus, or beginning to take their first steps with him as his followers. As we did this, they began to talk about the deep character flaws in their lives.

Carlos, who was a freshman in college at the time, and I spent hours together. He was bright and had an unusual zest for life. He struggled with some sexual addictions, and feared he would never be able to maintain a solid marriage. He and I would work through the issues, using the Bible as our reference. He would leave encouraged, but then he would pick up a prostitute on his way home. The next day he would be back, feeling devastated, and we would work through it all again. This went on for a couple of years, until finally I gave up. I felt I had nothing more to give him.

These two questions—what to do with all the people, and how to care for their inner struggles—weighed on our hearts. It struck me that Hebrews 3:13 contained the answer to what to do with our growing circle of friends. It says, "Encourage one another daily, as long as it is called Today, so that none of you may be hardened by sin's deceitfulness." It occurred to me that these new followers of Christ *could take care of one another*! It would take some daily intensity, and sufficient honesty to talk about sin's deceitfulness, but this was the answer we had sought.

Ken and I found that other references in the Bible reinforced this idea. One example was, "I myself am convinced, my brothers, that you yourselves are full of goodness, complete in knowledge and competent to instruct one another."[30] So we gathered our friends together, showed them what we had found in the Bible and told them to go find each other. We emphasized the importance of keeping the group small in order to maintain intimacy.

This approach also fit perfectly with the Brazilian ethos. Our Brazilian friends loved to hang out together in what they called a *turma*, which is a circle of friends that interacts in informal, spontaneous, and unscheduled ways. So what we suggested to them fit naturally with the culture.

There was still the question of Carlos and his inner battles with sexual temptation, not to mention many other people who struggled with other problems. By this time Carlos had a fiancée, and they connected with three other couples who met to study, pray, and talk. They also spent a lot of leisure time together. All of them were at about the same stage in their spiritual journey, and all of them had significant problems to overcome.

Some time later, Carlos graduated from the university, went into business and then married his fiancée. Over the next three years I had very little contact with them. Then one day as we walked together, Carlos made it a point to inform me that he had been faithful in his marriage. This was great news to me, and a pleasant surprise. It turns out that what had most helped him overcome his old habits was his closely knit group of friends.

What did those three equally immature, needy couples have to offer Carlos that I didn't? What I concluded was that they had accepted each other, even with all their weaknesses and flaws. They had a relationship in which it was safe to be honest. They created an environment of encouragement—a benign account-ability, a desire to not let each other down. In other words, integrity, love, humility, and forgiveness characterized their relationships. They experienced *koinonia*, which means holding *all things* in common. For Carlos to grow, it required more than just a one-on-one dialogue.

This happened in 1972. Carlos and his wife are still growing, as are their children. And, since then, this simple idea of turma has kept the message of Christ moving across Brazil through an organic relational network. The experience I just described is, in fact, a contemporary application of the oikos.

After about twenty-five years in Brazil, I moved my family back to the United States. We had become used to having friends that encouraged us to stay on track and persevere in our spiritual growth. We wondered if we would be able to find an equivalent of our Brazilian experience in Colorado.

I realized that it would be up to us to make it happen. We would need to find a few friends who would, for us, constitute a "household." The people we linked up with were often totally new to the whole idea of knowing God and following him. But they were willing to get together on a regular basis, to look at Scripture and discuss what it has to say about life.

In time, they became people with whom we could be trans-parent and vulnerable. This, of course, required trust, which always develops over time. Before long, a beautiful dynamic emerged despite our imperfections and struggles. And together we continue to grow today.

There is nothing exotic or complicated about what we're describing. Basically it involves a choice to engage a few of your friends in reading the Bible together and then encouraging one another to align your lives accordingly. To be meaningful, these relationships need to extend beyond the hour you might spend reading together. The conversations that occur in the casual, unstructured times, such as at a dinner table or on a ski slope, or during a trip to the mall, are often the most fruitful and enlightening. You don't have to add one more activity to your already full schedule; you just integrate and prioritize your relationships within the framework of your job and leisure. But in this context, you pursue one another in love. You make a conscious effort to be open, honest, truthful, nonjudgmental, forgiving, and humble. And you keep Jesus at the center of it all. It is amazing how this kind of mutual devotion can bring healing and joy.

An affair almost cost Brian his marriage. A business contract forced him to spend three months working in Chicago, away from home. While there, he met a woman who had just gone through a messy divorce. He listened to her story, and one thing led to another. They began to see each other every day.

When the job was over and it came time for him to return home, Brian had to face up to what he had done to his marriage. He was ashamed, and he didn't have the courage to return home. He thought about staying in Chicago. But one day, over the phone, he told his wife what was going on. The next few days were filled with shock and remorse as he fully realized what he had done.

Then Lynn, his wife, called and told Brian that she had been praying about what had happened. She said she would accept him back if he wanted to return. Brian was overwhelmed. He knew what kind of pain he had inflicted on her. To be forgiven was something he could not expect and did not deserve. But he accepted her invitation.

Brian knew all along that it was Lynn's faith in Christ that had enabled her to respond as she had. He had always respected that part of her life, but he had never taken it seriously for himself. Now he realized his need. A coworker he knew participated in a Bible study with some other businessmen on Friday mornings. Brian asked about it and was invited to join them. Soon the lights came on for him, and he opened his life to Christ. Over the next several months, friendships were forged with the other five guys in the study. He felt safe telling them the truth about his marriage.

Then Brian stopped showing up for the Friday morning meetings. One of the guys, Jeff, knew something was wrong. But instead of prying, he decided to just keep checking in. Finally Brian unloaded his story. The woman he had met in Chicago had called him to say she missed him. He was tempted by her call, which in turn made him feel ashamed. His rekindled struggle kept him from coming to the Friday meetings.

Once Brian got this news out in the open with Jeff, it all looked different to him. The temptation lost its attraction. The desire he had felt for the other woman turned to disgust. He felt free and clean. He was experiencing what the apostle John wrote about: "If we walk in the light, as he is in the light, we have fellowship with one another, and the blood of Jesus, his Son, purifies us from all sin."[31]

None of this could have happened if Brian hadn't been connected to a small group of friends who knew his personal story. When we bring our struggles out into the open with others who are walking with us in Christ, two things happen: Our friendships with one another deepen beyond belief, and the sins we are dealing with begin to lose their power over us.

The strange reality is that when we most need the support of a "Jeff" and a few others, the first tendency is to flee—to have an "early morning business appointment." Darkness is more comfortable than light when we're up to something we know is sin. So we withdraw from the very people who can most help us, exactly when we most need them. In this case, Jeff's friendship and personal attention saved a marriage.

Accept it: You will need honest help from your friends if you are to persevere over time in your journey with Christ. In our network of relationships, we need to imitate what Paul wrote to his friends in Ephesus: "Speaking the truth in love, we will in all things grow up into him who is the Head, that is, Christ. From him the whole body, joined and held together by every supporting ligament, grows and builds itself up in love, as each part does its work."[32]

As the life of Jesus inspires our relationships toward greater intimacy, others will naturally pay attention. Together we will become the personal seasoning in an impersonal world. And at the end of our days, we will know that we have lived a significant and meaningful life, a life that is about more than ourselves.

QUESTIONS FOR DISCUSSION

1. Why did Jesus focus so much of his time and attention on so few people? What was the vision that drove this? What can we learn from it?
2. Why do we need to be closely engaged with a few kindred spirits if we are to continue to make progress in our personal transformation?
3. Do you have the kind of people around you with whom you can give and receive spiritual support? If you do, how have these relationships been mutually beneficial? If you don't, what initiatives might you take to develop such an environment?

EPILOGUE

On our wedding day, in all our youthful naivete, my wife and I (Glenn) did at least one thing right: We made a decision that our togetherness would never be called into question, no matter what hardships we might face.

Since then we've experienced the same difficulties in life that most people face—financial uncertainty, the exhausting but rewarding job of raising children, emotional ups and downs, the deaths of close relatives, times of loneliness, and the ever-present demands of work.

After more than twenty-one years, our marriage is still strong and beautiful. There is not an ounce of doubt about the permanence of our relationship. We're not the most exciting and vivacious people in the world, but we make a good team. We have a very peaceful relationship. There is no power struggle between us, and therefore almost no conflict. Our values and beliefs are the same. We accept one another when we fail.

But the marriage is not perfect. The struggle in recent years has been to find time to enjoy life together the way we did when we were younger. The pressures of work and raising children can steal the spark and spontaneity from life. As a husband, I love my wife and kids so much that, for fear of making a painful mistake, I often fail to be decisive in big decisions. That can leave my wife feeling like she's in limbo. And there are days when a sullen mood gets the best of me, which saps life from her.

Nevertheless, our marriage has always been a refuge for our souls. If the world around us fell apart, we know that we would be standing together, arm-in-arm among the ruins. Musician Bruce Cockburn wrote lyrics that describe well what I feel about Michelle:

If this were the last night of the world
    what would I do?
What would I do that was different
    unless it was champagne with you?[1]

Our unity hinges on our mutual belief in God. We love because he loved us first. We forgive one another because he has forgiven us. As we each fix our eyes on Christ and follow him, he draws us together. His presence in our daily lives strengthens us and counsels us.

When we were first married, we decided that we would make Jesus and his Word the foundation and the North Star of our lives. He told a story about two men who built houses. One built on the sand and the other on a rock. Storms pounded them both equally hard, but only the house built on the rock was able to survive.

It's a story as simple as "The Three Little Pigs," but through this story Jesus made it clear that we all have to choose how and on what foundation we will build our lives. Life doesn't just happen. And the only basis strong enough to keep us from being swept away by life's difficulties, Jesus said, is a relationship with him and the application of his teaching.

In other words, the way you build a relationship — whether it be a marriage or a friendship — is to pay close attention to what Jesus says and then to put his words into action — depending on his strength as you build. His words are the bricks and mortar of life, but we have to do the bricklayer's work. We have to choose and act. If we anchor our lives in him, the storms won't destroy our souls or our relationships.

In this book, we've described what Jesus said and modeled about building healthy relationships—the four essential character traits. If, with God's involvement and inspiration, we would all build our lives on the basis of integrity, love, humility, and forgiveness, there would be dramatic growth. Our friendships and families would weather the storms.

The risk, however, is that one person in a relationship might decide not to follow Christ in the four essentials. And when that happens, everyone suffers. We know many single people who long to be married but who struggle to find a man or woman of integrity. They date, but can't seem to connect with a person who wants a permanent commitment. We know other people in marriages that are characterized by one-sided love: One spouse serves wholeheartedly, but the other doesn't reciprocate. We know people who have worked hard at developing a friendship only to see it collapse because of one person's selfishness. Others have been estranged for years because one person refuses to be humble and forgive.

God did not create us as people who, like computers, could be programmed to produce whole and healthy relationships. He gave us the freedom to choose and act. Without this freedom, sincere and authentic love would not be possible. But as a result, all relationships contain an element of unavoidable risk. One person's refusal to live according to the four essentials can undermine another person's best efforts to build a strong relationship.

More and more people today are unwilling to assume that risk. Many people are frustrated, disillusioned, and increasingly cynical about ever finding a whole relationship. There are so many bad stories circulating that people are afraid to write their *own* story.

If we think about Madelyn and Allan from chapter 9, we see the fragility inherent in all relationships. What started as a beautiful marriage gradually deteriorated as Allan drifted away from his responsibilities and commitment. The four essentials had almost vanished from their lives. Maybe you are in a relationship with a spouse or friend that languishes for the same reasons. Maybe, like Madelyn, you are suffering, dried up, exhausted, and afraid to try again. Perhaps you are doing your best to live with integrity and love, but the other person won't reciprocate.

What should you do when others don't respond positively to your best efforts?

Once again, we can look to Jesus as our model. He was the only person to perfectly live according to the four essentials, but most people rejected him. He knows all about what it means to love people; he gave his life only to be ridiculed and excluded. Amazingly, God knew beforehand that many would reject his love, but he sent his Son anyway.

Although his best efforts to love people were usually rebuffed, Jesus never stopped living according to the four essentials for whole relationships. Regardless of many negative results, Jesus did not fall away from his resolve to live a life characterized by integrity, love, humility, and forgiveness.

The life of Jesus teaches us that it is always right and good to live in accordance with the four essentials—*independent of the results*. This does not mean that we should risk our hearts in every relationship; we need discernment and wisdom. But integrity, love, humility, and forgiveness are *always* the most beautiful and noble way to live. These traits transcend all circumstances, all cultures, all generational fads. Jesus calls us to imitate him no matter the outcome.

The world desperately needs people who are being formed into the likeness of Christ, people who imitate him. The character traits he displayed for us are powerful to effect change. They are the only factors that can make joy, peace, and reconciliation between us possible. Through Jesus' life, these traits inject redemption and hope into a fragmented and despairing world. The more we become people of integrity, love, humility, and forgiveness, the more we will be people who restore meaning to an empty world.

Jesus showed us that even our best efforts can't *guarantee* perfect relationships, because the outcome depends on the decisions of the other people with whom we relate. But without the four essential character traits, the results will certainly be disastrous. The only hope of bringing about relational wholeness is for us to be absolutely committed to imitating Christ.

Therefore, we need to be people who are willing to take risks, to overcome our fears in order to bring hope and love to the people in our lives. With discernment and wisdom, we need to be people who are willing to grow in and live for Christ, to live for "more than me." That's the way he lived. He said that if we give ourselves to others in love, we will find abundant inner life.

Jesus does not ask us to live this way without promising to care for our deepest needs. As we go through the struggles of life, he will meet us, restore our souls, and use even the most painful experiences to bring about beauty. Jesus does not call us to such a life without promising to sustain us. He doesn't just throw us into the sea and tell us to swim.

Therefore we all have at least one relationship that is guaranteed, one person who will never leave us, reject us, or abandon us. He promises to walk with us through all hardships. And he is the one person we most need, the only one who can fulfill our deepest longings, and the only one who can carry us into eternity. By rooting our lives in him and trusting in his promises, we find the inner resources to love others even when they turn away.

The author of Hebrews offered these words to help us persevere: "Let us fix our eyes on Jesus, the author and perfecter of our faith, who for the joy set before him endured the cross, scorning its shame, and sat down at the right hand of the throne of God. Consider him who endured such opposition from sinful men, so that you will not grow weary and lose heart."[2]

NOTES

1. 1 Corinthians 13:2, emphasis added.
2. Glenn Tinder, *Against Fate: An Essay on Personal Dignity* (Notre Dame, IN: University of Notre Dame Press, 1981).
3. Robert Reich, *The Future of Success: Working and Living in the New Economy* (New York: Vintage, 2002), 7, 9.
4. Al Gini, *My Job, My Self: Work and the Creation of the Modern Individual* (New York: Routledge, 2001), 202.
5. Douglas Noll quoted in Ellen Wulfhorst, "Religion finds firm footing in some offices," Reuters, December 6, 2006, http://www.reuters.com/article/ousiv/idUSN0531418620061206.
6. Gini, 202.
7. *About Schmidt*, directed by Alexander Payne (New York: Avery Pix and New Line Cinema, 2002).
8. *Contact*, directed by Robert Zemeckis (South Side Amusement Company and Warner Brothers Pictures, 1997).
9. Personal interview, 2003.
10. Neil Howe and William Strauss, *Millennials Rising* (New York: Vintage, 2000), 35.
11. Howe and Strauss, 204.
12. Howe and Strauss, 123.
13. Ethan Watters, *Urban Tribes* (New York: Bloomsbury, 2003), 28.

14. Watters, 8.
15. Watters, 18.
16. Watters, 54–55.

Chapter 2

1. C. S. Lewis, *The Weight of Glory and Other Addresses* (New York: HarperCollins, 2001), 32–33.
2. John 17:24.
3. Genesis 1:26, emphasis added.
4. John 16:15.
5. Kenneth Scott Latourette, *A History of Christianity* (Peabody, MA: Prince Press, 2003), 1:145.
6. See 1 Corinthians 12.
7. Luke 22:42.
8. George Perkins, et al, *The American Tradition in Literature*, 6th ed. (New York: Random House, 1985), 2:11.
9. Ralph Waldo Emerson, "Self-Reliance," in *The American Tradition in Literature*, 6th ed., ed. George Perkins, et al (New York: Random House, 1985), 1:844.
10. Emerson, 848.
11. Emerson, 851.
12. Walt Whitman, "Song of Myself," in *The American Tradition in Literature*, 6th ed., ed. George Perkins, et al (New York: Random House, 1985), 27–63.
13. Robert Bellah, Richard Madsen, William Sullivan, Ann Swidler, and Steven Tipton, *Habits of the Heart* (New York: Harper & Row, 1985), 107.
14. John 17:20-23, emphasis added.

Chapter 3

1. Psalm 19:1-4.
2. Psalm 8:3-4, MSG.

3. Gerald Schroeder, *The Science of God: The Convergence of Scientific and Biblical Wisdom* (New York: Broadway Books, 1998), 5.

4. Lee Strobel, *The Case for a Creator* (Grand Rapids, MI: Zondervan, 2004), 168–169, 171.

5. Schroeder, 177.

6. Patrick Glynn, *God: The Evidence: The Reconciliation of Faith and Reason in a Post-Secular World* (Roseville, CA: Prima Publishing, 1999), 22, 25, emphasis added.

7. Genesis 12:2-3.

8. Deuteronomy 4:6-7, emphasis added.

9. Romans 1:24.

10. Jeremiah 4:18.

11. Matthew 27:46.

12. Francis Schaeffer, "The Purpose of Our Creation Fulfilled," *A Series of L'Abri Lectures*, No. 12.

13. John 3:16.

14. Ephesians 2:19,22; 4:1.

15. Rodney Stark, *The Rise of Christianity: How the Obscure, Marginal Jesus Movement Became the Dominant Religious Force in the Western World in a Few Centuries* (New York: HarperCollins, 1996), 208, 211.

16. Stark, 211–212, 215.

17. Francis S. Collins, *The Language of God: A Scientist Presents Evidence for Belief* (New York: Free Press, 2006), 11, 13, 15–16.

18. Collins, 19–20.

19. Collins, 20.

20. Collins, 21.

21. Annie Dillard, *Teaching a Stone to Talk: Expeditions and Encounters* (New York: Harper Perennial, 1992), 138.

22. Dillard, 139.

Chapter 4

1. Ephesians 2:6.
2. Ephesians 4:23-24, emphasis added.
3. Ephesians 5:1-2, emphasis added.
4. Ephesians 4:2, emphasis added.
5. Philippians 2:5-8, emphasis added.
6. Ephesians 4:32, emphasis added.
7. For the full account of Jacob's encounter with God, see Genesis 32:24-31. For the account of Moses, see Exodus 34:29-35.
8. Genesis 18:25.
9. Isaiah 5:16.
10. Psalm 96:13.
11. Psalm 97:2.
12. See Exodus 32:7-14.
13. Deuteronomy 7:8-9, emphasis added.
14. Philippians 2:5-8.
15. 1 Peter 2:24.
16. Dorothy Sayers, *The Mind of the Maker* (San Francisco: HarperSanFrancisco, 1979), 7.
17. Hebrews 1:3.

Chapter 5

1. Dick Keyes, "Image and Reality in Society," *What in the World Is Real? Challenging the Superficial in Today's World* (Champaign, IL: Communications Institute and L'Abri Fellowship, 1982), 82.
2. John Adams quoted in David McCullough, *John Adams* (New York: Simon & Schuster, 2001), 289.
3. Stephen L. Carter, "The Insufficiency of Honesty," *The Atlantic Monthly*, February 1996, 74–76.
4. Carter, 74.
5. Glenn Tinder, "Can We Be Good Without God?"

The Atlantic Monthly, December 1989, 69.

6. Transparency International, "FAQ," http://www.transparency.org/news_room/faq/corruption_faq.

7. Marcelo Abreu, trans. Glenn McMahan, "Cleaning employee at Brasilia Airport finds bag with $10,000," *Correio Braziliense*, March 12, 2004, http://www.consciencia.net/2004/mes/03/honestidade.html.

8. Daniela Pinheiro, trans. Glenn McMahan, "Lie, because I like it!" *Veja*, October 18, 2006, 11–15.

9. Keyes, 75.

10. Ernest Becker, "The Fragile Fiction," *The Truth about Truth: Deconfusing and Re-constructing the Postmodern World*, ed. Walter Truett Anderson (New York: Putnam, 1995), 34–35.

11. *The Talented Mr. Ripley*, directed by Anthony Minghella (Paramount Pictures and Miramax Films, 1999).

12. John 6:56-57.

13. John 6:66.

14. Matthew 23:27-28.

15. Matthew 26:38-39.

16. John 18:30.

17. John 18:31.

18. John 18:38.

19. For the complete story of Jesus' trial, see Luke 22–23.

Chapter 6

1. See Mark 12:30-31.

2. 1 John 4:10, emphasis added.

3. Luke 23:42-43, NASB, emphasis added.

4. 1 John 4:18, NASB.

5. Steve McMorran, "Everest pioneer condemns leaving climber to die," *Pittsburgh Post-Gazette*, May 25, 2006, http://www.post-gazette.com/pg/06145/692954-82.stm.

6. McMorran.

7. Matthew 22:39.

8. Charles S. Houston, MD, "What Happens at Altitude," in Broughton Coburn, *Everest: Mountain Without Mercy* (Washington, DC: MacGillivray Freeman Films/National Geographic Society, 1997), 123.

9. Coburn, 120.

10. Steve McMorran, "Hillary rips climbers who left a dying man," USAToday.com, May 24, 2006, http://www.usatoday.com/news/world/2006-05-24-everest-pioneer_x.htm.

11. 1 Corinthians 13:2.

12. Stephen Kanitz, trans. Glenn McMahan, "Family in first place," *Veja*, February 20, 2002, 26.

13. Kanitz, 26.

14. See John 10:10.

15. Luke 9:23, NASB.

16. Luke 9:24-25, NASB.

17. Song of Solomon 4:10-11,14-15, NASB.

18. Song of Solomon 4:16, NASB.

19. Edward T. Hall, *The Hidden Dimension* (Garden City, NY: Doubleday, 1966).

20. Exodus 20:3.

21. John Gottman, *Why Marriages Succeed or Fail: And How You Can Make Yours Last* (New York: Simon & Schuster), 142–144.

22. Ephesians 5:25,27.

Chapter 7

1. The American Association of Variable Star Observers, June 14, 2007, http://www.aavso.org/vstar/vsots/1200.shtml.

2. Gerald Schroeder, *The Science of God* (New York: Broadway Books, 1997), 185.

3. Schroeder, 128.

4. Romans 3:24, emphasis added.

5. Romans 3:27.

6. Frederick Buechner, *The Magnificent Defeat* (New York: HarperCollins, 1985), 18.

7. Buechner, 134–135.

8. Stanley Fish, "Why We Can't Just Get Along," *The New York Times*, October 29, 2006, http://fish.blogs.nytimes.com/2006/10/29/why-we-cant-just-get-along/.

9. John Gottman, *Why Marriages Succeed or Fail: And How You Can Make Yours Last* (New York: Simon & Schuster, 1994), 73.

10. Gottman, 79.

11. Gottman, 84–90.

12. Gottman, 94–95.

13. Daniel Gilbert, "He who cast the first stone probably didn't," *The International Herald Tribune*, July 24, 2006, http://www.iht.com/articles/2006/07/24/opinion/edgilbert.php.

14. See Matthew 7:3-5.

15. C. S. Lewis, *Mere Christianity* (San Francisco: HarperSanFrancisco, 2001), 128.

16. Bruce Cockburn, "Cry of a Tiny Babe," *Nothing But a Burning Light* (New York: Columbia Records, 1991).

17. See Matthew 5:3-6.

18. See Matthew 5:7-9.

19. See Matthew 5:10.

20. Jim Collins, *Good to Great* (New York: HarperCollins, 2001), 21.

21. Collins, 26.

22. See John 8:1-11.

23. Glenn Tinder, *Against Fate: An Essay on Personal Dignity* (South Bend, IN: University of Notre Dame Press, 1981), 20.

24. Psalm 7:15, NASB.

Chapter 8

1. Thiago Velloso, trans. Glenn McMahan, "Guerra de famílias," *Revista Terra*, No. 143, March 2004, 70–77.
2. Ana Claudia Marques, trans. Glenn McMahan, "Política e questão de família," *Revista de Antropologia*, University of São Paulo, 45, No. 2 (2002), 417–442.
3. Bureau of Justice Statistics, U.S. Department of Justice, "Homicide Victimization, 1950–2005," http://www.ojp. usdoj.gov/bjs/homicide/tables/totalstab.htm (accessed June 28, 2007).
4. See Matthew 18:23-27, NASB.
5. Miroslav Volf, *Exclusion and Embrace: A Theological Exploration of Identity, Otherness, and Reconciliation* (Nashville: Abingdon, 1996), 9.
6. Matthew 18:32-33.
7. Matthew 18:34-35.
8. Romans 3:22.
9. Romans 8:1.
10. Ephesians 5:28-29.
11. See Matthew 19:3-9.
12. See John 2:24-25.
13. Jeremiah 3:1,12-13, NASB.
14. Ephesians 4:32.
15. Paul Tournier, *Guilt and Grace* (New York: Harper & Row, 1958), 100.
16. Volf, 292.
17. Hebrews 9:27.
18. See Romans 8:1.
19. Romans 12:19, NASB.
20. Volf, 298.
21. 1 Peter 2:23, emphasis added.
22. Revelation 21:3-4.

Chapter 9

1. Ephesians 4:32–5:2.
2. Mark Edmundson, "Who's Your Daddy?" *The New York Times*, September 23, 2007, http://www.nytimes.com/2007/09/23/opinion/23edmundson.html.
3. I am indebted to one of my clients for this very helpful analogy.
4. John Gottman, *Why Marriages Succeed or Fail: And How You Can Make Yours Last* (New York: Simon & Schuster, 1994), 166.
5. Gottman, 167.
6. Gottman, 168.
7. Gottman, 181, 183.
8. See Romans 3:20.
9. Romans 8:3, emphasis added.
10. Romans 7:24-25.

Chapter 10

1. Matthew 5:3-6.
2. Wim Rietkerk, "God Bless America," *The International Newsletter of L'Abri Fellowship* (Rochester, MN: L'Abri International, 2006), 5–6.
3. C. S. Lewis, *Voyage of the Dawn Treader* (New York: Macmillan, 1952), 75–76.
4. Lewis, *Voyage*, 93.
5. Ephesians 4:13.
6. Ephesians 1:3.
7. Ephesians 2:8-9.
8. See Romans 8:16.
9. Romans 8:31,37.
10. C. S. Lewis, *Mere Christianity* (SanFrancisco: HarperSanFrancisco, 2001), 192.
11. See Romans 7:5,17,20,23; Galatians 5:16-18.

12. Romans 7:21-23.
13. Psalm 139:23-24.
14. Hebrews 4:12.
15. Hebrews 12:7,11, emphasis added.
16. John 14:26.
17. Psalm 11:1.
18. 1 Corinthians 2:10-11.
19. 1 Corinthians 2:9-10.
20. 2 Corinthians 3:3, emphasis added.
21. 2 Corinthians 12:9.
22. Romans 12:2.
23. Aldous Huxley, *Ends and Means* (New York: Harper & Brothers, 1939), 314, 316.
24. John 8:32.

Chapter 11

1. Paul Tournier, *The Gift of Feeling* (Atlanta: John Knox, 1979), 2–4.
2. Tournier, 5–6.
3. Romans 12:10,15-16.
4. 1 Thessalonians 5:11.
5. Galatians 5:13.
6. John 6:15.
7. See John 6:66.
8. See Luke 7:38.
9. See John 11:33-36.
10. Acts 2:46.
11. Robert Banks, *Paul's Idea of Community* (Peabody, MA: Hendrickson, 1994), 42.
12. Acts 16:15, emphasis added.
13. Acts 16:30-32,34, emphasis added.
14. See 1 Timothy 3, for example.
15. Acts 20:20, emphasis added.

16. Colossians 1:10.
17. Rodney Stark, *The Rise of Christianity* (Princeton, NJ: Princeton University Press, 1996; paperback edition, San Francisco: HarperSanFrancisco, 1997), 74.
18. Stark, *Rise of Christianity*, 82–83.
19. Stark, *Rise of Christianity*, 90.
20. Banks, 56.
21. 1 John 1:7.
22. 1 John 1:7.
23. 1 John 1:7.
24. Banks, 56.
25. Paul Johnson, *A History of Christianity* (New York: Simon & Schuster, 1976), 103.
26. Rodney Stark, *For the Glory of God* (Princeton, NJ: Princeton University Press, 2003), 34.
27. Stark, *Glory of God*, 33.
28. Stark, *Glory of God*, 40.
29. Romans 12:10.
30. Romans 15:14.
31. 1 John 1:7.
32. Ephesians 4:15-16.

Epilogue
1. Bruce Cockburn, "The Last Night of the World," *Breakfast in New Orleans, Dinner in Timbuktu* (Golden Mountain Music Corp., 1999).
2. Hebrews 12:2-3.

ABOUT THE
AUTHORS

JIM PETERSEN is an associate to the general director of The Navigators. In 1963 the Petersens moved to Brazil, where they began by working with university students, helping them develop a deeper understanding of Scripture as it applied to their careers and families. This, in time, expanded into a movement that spread across Brazil. In 1972, Jim began to be involved internationally. From 1986 to 2000, he served as a vice president on the international executive team of The Navigators. In those years, he coached people working in the Middle East, Europe, Asia, Africa, and Latin America. Having lived and worked in many cultures, Jim has acquired a wealth of experience in communicating biblical truth to people who are normally outside the Christian context. He shares what he has learned in his books, *Living Proof, Church Without Walls, Lifestyle Discipleship,* and *The Insider* (coauthored with Mike Shamy). Jim and his wife, Marge, have raised four children and live in Colorado Springs, Colorado.

GLENN MCMAHAN and his wife, Michelle, have mentored Brazilian university students and business professionals since 1995, using the Scriptures as a basis for discussions about family relationships, work, and spiritual growth. They have enjoyed opening their home to hundreds of Brazilian friends from around the country. Glenn also holds discussion groups for people interested in investigating the intellectual basis for the Christian faith. Prior to his move to Brazil, Glenn worked as a newspaper reporter in Maryland and Washington, DC, covering politics and education. He holds a master's degree in journalism from the University of Maryland. He and Michelle live with their two sons in the state of Paraná, Brazil.

DR. DAVID RUSS is a licensed psychologist and president of Carolinas Counseling Group in Charlotte, North Carolina. He has taught courses at various seminaries and universities and has been practicing clinical psychology for more than twenty years. In 1992, David received his PhD in psychology from Georgia State University. He lives with his wife, Linda, and their three children in Charlotte, North Carolina.

Check out more great titles from NavPress!

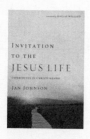

Invitation to the Jesus Life
Jan Johnson
978-1-60006-146-2

1-60006-146-X

It's easy to learn a little something about Jesus, but to encounter him on a daily basis changes everything. No longer can we live with the same earthly behavior or attitude. Our focus becomes eternal. Jan Johnson helps you experience Jesus in such a way that his love-drenched, others-focused nature shapes you character.

Coffeehouse Theology
Ed Cyzewski
978-1-60006-277-3

1-60006-277-6

A relationship with God is central to life-breathing theology, but today's culture experiences a barrier of ignorance and misunderstanding of the church's mission. Through stories and illustrations, Ed Cyzewski builds a method for theology that is rooted in a relationship with God and his mission.

How Can a Good God Let Bad Things Happen?
Mark Tabb
978-1-60006-268-1

1-60006-268-7

In a world where tragedy and catastrophe strike daily, God's people pray for blessings but feel abandoned. Author Mark Tabb takes readers through the story of Job to show that God has not forsaken us.

Here's a resource
to help you pray
with more

Power,
Passion,
& Purpose